At 39, Karl Kaiser has spent his working years studying, teaching and writing on economics and political science. With a doctorate from the University of Cologne, after postgraduate work at Oxford and the University of Grenoble, Kaiser lectured at Harvard and was a Research Associate at that university's Center for International Affairs. He subsequently taught at the University of Bonn, at the Johns Hopkins Center at Bologna, Italy, and he returned to the U.S. as Visiting Professor of Government at Harvard.

He is now Professor of Political Science at the University of the Saar in Saarbruecken, West Germany. Kaiser is Chairman of the German Society of Peace and Conflict Research and a member of the Federal German Council of Environmental Advisors.

He is the author of *EEC and Free Trade Area, England and the Continent in European Integration, German Foreign Policy in Transition, Bonn Between East and West, Peace Research in the Federal Republic of Germany, Britain and Germany: Changing Societies and the Future of Foreign Policy.* He has contributed to such journals as *Europa-Archiv, International Organization, World Politics, Political Science Quarterly, The World Today.*

EUROPE
AND
THE UNITED STATES

The Future of the Relationship

by
Karl Kaiser

Library of Congress Catalog Card No. 73-75612
SBN 910416-18-4

This book was set in Helvetica by Hendricks-Miller Typographic Co., and printed and bound by Columbia Planograph Co.

Price: $2.50 (paper) $3.95 (cloth)

Columbia Books, Inc., Publishers
Washington, DC
1973

To
Andreas and Markus

PREFACE

The United States and Europe have a unique relationship. Their community of purposes, flowing from similar cultural and philosophic values, is essential to world peace and development.

The Atlantic relationship stimulates freedom and diversity of approach in many parts of the world. It permits the United States and Europe to advance a policy of détente with Moscow and Peking. The *Ostpolitik* of the Federal Republic of Germany is anchored in European-American cooperation.

Notwithstanding the philosophic and policy imperatives of the Atlantic relationship, abrasive problems have emerged in recent years to disturb European-American perspectives. Monetary, trade, and security problems have become divisive, and a shrill tone has characterized recent European-American negotiations.

What is now required of political leadership in the United States and Europe is vision, courage, and willingness to act in harmony with the overarching social and cultural challenges of our times. Narrow economic and financial interests must not be allowed to hack away at great Atlantic purposes. Prompt and constructive measures are essential not only in the interest of the Atlantic area but also for the peace of the world and the advancement of peoples in less-developed countries.

With these problems and perspectives in mind and with a view to the governmental negotiations which must take place in 1973 and thereafter, a conference was held in Columbia, Maryland (near Washington, D. C.), December 7-10, 1972. European and U.S. parliamentarians, government officials, scholars, specialists in the mass media, and business leaders participated. The December meeting was the culmination of a process which began months earlier in Europe. In an effort to establish European objectives and policies related to the United States, four separate national groups met in June and July, 1972, in

Bonn, Paris, London, and Rome. In October, 1972, an all-European meeting took place in Bonn.

These discussions were aided by a policy paper, written by Professor Karl Kaiser of the University of the Saarland. During the summer of 1972, Professor Kaiser was a Scholar-in-Residence at the Aspen Institute for Humanistic Studies in Aspen, Colorado, where he had an opportunity to discuss European views with American and European leaders of thought. Professor Kaiser's paper, revised after the December conference to reflect discussions at the meeting, follows this preface, and constitutes this book.

The Aspen Institute and the International Association for Cultural Freedom, which is based in Paris, sponsored the entire project. It is our hope that these conferences will be part of a continuing educational process which stimulates both governmental action and public debate.

The project was made possible by support from the Aspen Institute and a grant from the Alfried Krupp von Bohlen und Halbach Foundation.

We wish to express our gratitude to the donors and to all those who participated in the discussions held in Europe and the United States. We are especially grateful to Robert O. Anderson, Chairman of the Aspen Institute, and Sir Alan Bullock, Chairman of the International Association for Cultural Freedom, for acting as co-chairmen of the Columbia conference.

Finally, our deep appreciation goes to Professor Kaiser for his scholarly and imaginative work.

Shepard Stone
President, International Association
for Cultural Freedom

J. E. Slater
President, Aspen Institute
for Humanistic Studies

December 1972

TABLE OF CONTENTS

Page

1
INTRODUCTION

In 1976 the American people will celebrate the bicentennial anniversary of their nation's founding. As they contemplate its past achievements and its future, the international community, along with the United States, will be in the midst of the most crucial period since the early post-war years.

Basic structural elements of the international system which emerged in the wake of World War II have undergone profound change. Old adversary relationships are developing cooperative dimensions; old friendships are experiencing abrasive tensions. New power centers are emerging while old ones are redefining their roles. The international economy is in such a critical state that formerly valid solutions have become inadequate. Some developments which offer new elements for cooperation in certain areas render more difficult the maintenance of security in others. Hence, the stage is set for a period of important decisions, uncertainties, and potential instabilities.

The decisions taken in the next few years by the major actors in the international system will in all likelihood determine whether the remaining decades of this century will be characterized by moderation, absence of war, and peaceful change, or whether we will enter a period of economic and political instability. Indeed, as has been rightly remarked,[1] the present constellation of East-West politics comes as close as one can imagine to being the functional equivalent of a peace treaty marking the end of World War II.

The 1972 presidential elections in the United States provide an opportune moment for Americans and Euro-

---

[1] François Duchêne, "A New European Defense Community," *Foreign Affairs,* October, 1971, pp. 69-82.

peans to review the future together. It is during the next American Administration that most critically important decisions will be made, by the United States, the governments of Western Europe, and other nations.

Many events in 1973 will place Europe at the center of international diplomacy: the European Conference for Security and Cooperation; negotiations on a Mutual Balanced Force Reduction with the Socialist states; and negotiations on international economic reform, in which the European Community, along with Japan, will be the main partner of the United States.

It is the purpose of this book to set forth a European position in regard to the major issues which confront both Europe and America. In formulating opinions, I have tried as nearly as possible to reflect European points of view. This task would have been impossible without the experience of five meetings with distinguished politicians, intellectuals, and personalities of public life in different European countries and without individual comments which I have received from various Europeans.

I am deeply grateful for the advice and active participation of these Europeans and of the Americans who attended the conference held at Columbia, Maryland, in December, 1972. (The names of participants are given in an appendix.)

My special thanks go to the Aspen Institute for Humanistic Studies and the International Association for Cultural Freedom for having organized and supported this unprecedented exercise in intra-European and trans-Atlantic dialogue.

Despite my best efforts to set forth European opinions on the issues covered in this book, the views expressed herein necessarily also reflect my own personal views. For this, I am alone responsible.

Karl Kaiser
University of the Saarland
66 Saarbruecken
West Germany

2
COMPONENTS OF CHANGE IN THE PRESENT INTERNATIONAL SYSTEM

During recent years various statesmen and scholars have, on various occasions, proclaimed the end of the post-war period. What used to be a subject for dispute is now a matter of consensus. Judging by the scope of change, we have arrived at a turning point of post-war politics which heralds the emergence of a new international system. What are the most important of these changes and what dilemmas do they pose, particularly regarding the future of European-American relations?

The first structural change consists of the new role played by multinational politics or transnational relations which complement, interact with, and, indeed, change traditional interstate relations. Multinational politics results from transnational interaction between different societies, such as the free movement of goods, investment, or persons. With the increasing accessibility of liberal Western societies to the outside world, transnational relations have grown spectacularly, as the growth of international investment, trade, and movement of persons demonstrates.

States can influence these processes, but they cannot completely master them, for they take place in a transnational milieu that partially eludes governmental control. Many of the critical developments in the international economy today are, in fact, due to transnational relations, *e.g.,* in the field of monetary or investment relations.

Behind the present strains and crises in the international economy, therefore, is a structural problem. Between the option of cutting off economic, social, or scientific transnational links with the outside world, which would be self-defeating, and the choice of acting alone, which would be ultimately futile, governments have only one option, namely, to coordinate policies in a number of areas increasingly vital to the well-being of modern societies.

In this expanding transnational milieu of interdependence the classical patterns of interstate behavior become obsolete. As in the nuclear game, gains in many areas of international economic policy are no longer made at someone else's expense; rather, gains—and losses—are shared by all. At a time when most Western governments are turning inward to face critical domestic problems, their societies are interfering with each other more than ever.[1]

A problem of considerable magnitude is thus posed: in many of the areas now on the agenda of international economic reform genuine progress will be possible only if we abandon past methods of interstate economic diplomacy and raise governmental relations to a qualitatively new level of policy coordination. Obviously, such a course will raise extraordinary difficulties, but, without a new and effective system of international management, the present strains in international economic relations are bound to become worse and to threaten not only international prosperity but also the Western system of cooperation and security which has been built since World War II.

The changing character of East-West relations, for more than two decades the dominant element of tension in world politics, constitutes a second area of structural transformation in contemporary international politics. To be sure these changes have not come about suddenly. But developments in the past two or three years suggest that there are now new opportunities to place East-West relations on a qualitatively new level, where cooperative

---

[1] These problems are examined more closely in my "Transnational Politics: Toward a Theory of Multinational Politics," *International Organization*, Autumn 1971 (Vol. 25, No. 4), pp. 790-817; and Robert O. Keohane and Joseph S. Nye, Jr., eds., *Transnational Relations and World Politics* (Cambridge, Mass.: Harvard University Press, 1972).

frameworks will moderate and perhaps eventually change the antagonistic nature of the relationship.

The American-Soviet agreements concluded during President Nixon's last visit to Moscow affirm a common responsibility to contain conflict and advance cooperation in the area of arms control and in a number of other areas vital to both countries. In Europe, West Germany's Ostpolitik, benefited by general support from Germany's American and European allies and complemented by the Four Power Agreement on Berlin, has led to settlement of what used to be Europe's potentially most explosive problems. Mutual recognition of the status quo by West Germany, the Soviet Union, and East Germany, along with negotiations and agreements between the two German states, have opened the way to normalization of relationships and cooperation in an arena which was once the focus of the Cold War. The process set in motion at the level of the superpowers and by West European and West German diplomacy will now enter a new phase, with multilateral negotiations on force reductions, other arms control measures and cooperation on all items on the agenda of a forthcoming European Conference on Security and Cooperation.

But any process designed to change an international structure which has existed for over 20 years and has shaped policies and attitudes raises new problems while solving old ones. The inevitable bilateralism between the United States and the Soviet Union on certain matters, arising out of their special responsibilities and strengths, will be difficult to reconcile with the necessities of multilateralism: maintaining effective working relationships within the Western Alliance. In both East and West, the lessening need for ideological and political unity may unleash social and political forces which challenge political structures, set in motion processes that exceed the limits of gradualism in the transformation of East-West relations, and thereby threaten stability.

It is clear that current changes in East-West relations not only offer new opportunities for achieving stability and peace but also challenge participating states to guide this process prudently.

The present reassessment of American foreign policy signals a third structural change in international politics. After three decades of far-reaching and costly involvement in every corner of the globe, the United States is re-examining its world role. Although the tragic experience of the Vietnam War has undoubtedly accelerated this process, it is likely that the reassessment would have occurred in any case. The high cost of overseas involve-ment, the urgent need for domestic reforms, and a general mood of withdrawal from over-commitment in the world constitute strong pressures on the American Administra-tion to re-examine American foreign policy.

Most Europeans see President Nixon's reelection as reflecting a popular mandate for prudent internationalism and for gradualism in a reassessment of America's inter-national role. But there is little doubt that the redefi-nition of this role had already begun in President Nixon's first term. The Nixon Doctrine quite clearly expresses America's desire for other power centers and states to play a stronger role in maintaining world security, with the United States exercising continued—but reduced—responsibilities for preserving international stability and order.

It is this meaning—and not the often and easily refuted mechanistic revival of a bygone world—that one should read into Administration pronouncements on the useful-ness of a balance of power and of a world in which five centers of power help preserve peace. Most Europeans regard America's efforts to stabilize U.S.-Soviet relations and increase cooperation between East and West while cautiously preserving her alliance with Europe—as the only sensible way of approaching the future.

The absence of a ready-made American blueprint for reorganization of relations among Europeans and between

Americans and Europeans, sometimes criticized as marking a shift toward an ambivalent American policy governed exclusively by U.S. national interests, has its positive side. To Europeans it signals the end of a period in which the United States provided the answers for others, and offers an opportunity to join with the United States in developing policies for a stable world order.

Changes on the international scene and in American policy raise, therefore, a series of important questions to be faced together by the United States and Europe. Of paramount importance is the problem of how to reform the international economic system so that strains in this field will not affect security relationships. Second, the United States and Europe will have to examine together a host of problems which arise from their common desire to restructure relations in Europe in ways which will give a greater role to Western Europe and improve conditions for peace in that area. Any such examination will necessarily include reassessment of their mutual security relationship with a view to maintaining stability in Europe while at the same time allowing for peaceful change.

In Europe the entry of Britain and other states into the European Community marks a new phase in the reemergence of the Western sector from the debacles of nationalism, World War II and decolonialization. We see emerging one of the largest and most prosperous political units in the world. To be sure, this grouping has not yet moved beyond the first stages of economic integration toward the goal of political unity but the course is undoubtedly set in that direction. Moreover, the need for a new system of managing the interdependent international economy will increasingly force members of the Community to arrive at a common point of view when dealing with the United States and Japan. The new round of negotiations on arms control and measures of cooperation between East and West will also motivate Community members to coordinate their policies.

The rise of China and Japan should be mentioned as a final important structural change in international politics. Both will play an increasingly vital role in Asia and throughout the world. Japan's contribution to international economic reform and her cooperation with the European Community and the United States are vital to any new system of managing the international economy. Beyond this Europe should make every possible effort to preserve and enhance Japan's membership in a broader Western system of cooperation.

On the other hand, the implications for Europe and European-American relations of China's rise cannot easily be ascertained. Although Western European efforts to play China off against the Soviet Union are unlikely to strengthen European security, the question still remains as to what practical conclusions follow from Europe's and China's identical desire to prevent superpower condominium, particularly Soviet hegemony.

The tasks ahead for both Europe and the United States will not be easy. In the area of security they must reconcile the goal of Western European unity and a peaceful transformation of East-West relations in Europe with a viable, reorganized security relationship between North America and Western Europe. In the economic field they must organize their competing and complementary interest within a new international system of management which is appropriate to the interdependent realities of today and which transcends the obsolete patterns of interstate diplomacy.

3
RESTRUCTURING ATLANTIC RELATIONS AND INTERNATIONAL POLITICS

The preceding analysis of contemporary international politics suggests that the next few years can be used to create the conditions for a moderate and peaceful international system in the remaining decades of this century. Or, owing to short-sighted policies or mere inaction, the post-war international system—which brought liberty to many peoples, which made possible unprecedented (though unevenly distributed) prosperity, and which prevented large-scale war throughout the world except Asia—will lapse into an inherently unstable state of multiple imbalances and excessive competition, without adequate machinery for regulating conflicts or reducing risks.

In modern history, periods with potential for reconstructing international politics have usually followed wars and major upheavals. The present opportunity occurs without such prior events. (American involvement in Vietnam has only accelerated a change in American foreign policy which would have occurred in any case.) As a result, pressures of time and stress are less pronounced and the turmoil of change is not quite so turbulent as in earlier periods.

While such a state of affairs may be grounds for moderate optimism, statesmen in the West today face a more difficult task than their predecessors during the period of reconstruction between 1945 and 1950. First, unlike those who were "present at the Creation," today's decision-makers do not benefit from the unifying effect of global struggle with the Soviet Union. The contemporary world has more actors, and these actors must be dealt with in complex relationships which combine competition with cooperation. Second, decisions on a number of important problems can no longer be taken by the United States alone; participation by many partners in decision-making and policy implementation is an essential precondition for success today.

Finally, given the basic nature of today's multinational politics of interdependence, states must seek solutions which integrate the various interconnecting realms of security, diplomacy, trade, and finance. Although the problem areas identified on the following pages are examined separately and consecutively, they are issues which, in fact, policy must integrate.

1. The Politics of International Economic Reform

Crossroads Ahead

It is obvious that nothing causes as many strains in contemporary European-American relations as economic problems. Less obvious is the fact that preservation of the international economic system developed after World War II is at stake. This system faces disruption and, with it, the prosperity, stability, and political cooperation which arose in its wake.

Immediate remedies for the economic strains in European-American relations are a paramount task of statesmanship but any steps taken will ultimately be futile if they are not carried out in the context of the broader international economy dominated by America, Europe, and Japan.

The global economy may well be brought down by its own success. The post-war attempt at rebuilding the international economy through reconstruction, liberalization of trade, and an effective monetary system has produced extraordinary results. World exports rose from $60 billion in 1950 to $310 billion in 1970; the real GNP in the Organization for Economic Cooperation and Development (OECD) countries rose from $836 billion in 1950 to $2,012 billion in 1970. The world today enjoys unprecedented volume and freedom in the movement of goods and persons, in sharing technology and ideas, and in mutual assistance.

The result has been an interdependent and interwoven international economy. This did not emerge accidentally; it was, rather, a deliberate objective of the statesmen who laid the groundwork for reconstruction of the post-war international economy. But the price of such interdependence is constant interference into one another's affairs. A decision by the American President may threaten employment in another continent. An action by European central banks may upset the economic policy of the United States. Investment decisions by private corporations or speculative money movements by private banks may neutralize the policy of several governments simultaneously.

Nation-states remain the ultimate units of decision-making in international politics, but they are no longer able to control transnational forces. In addition, since welfare states can no longer afford to be indifferent to oscillations of economic trends and since, as democratic states, they must be sensitive to popular demands and reactions, tensions obviously arise between the new transnational reality of economics and the national inability to master it.

Two opposing conclusions are being drawn from the emergence of this multinational, interdependent economy.

States can, first, reverse this process and protect themselves from the undesirable effects of transnational freedom of movement by encapsulating themselves, erecting barriers, and imposing restrictions on the movement of goods, persons, investments, etc. In America, Western Europe, and Japan we have observed instances of this kind. But actions of this kind cannot be carried out in isolation: they tend to set loose a chain of counter-reactions on the part of other states participating in the interdependent economic system. Herein lies the real danger of such self-defeating reactions against interdependence, as witnessed in certain external measures taken by the United States in August, 1971, and protectionist measures taken by the European Community and Japan. They are not far from triggering a downward process reminiscent of the "beggar my neighbor" policies of the 1920's and 1930's which could well wreck the reconstruction of the international economy after the War.

The second conclusion which can be drawn from the emergence of a multinational economy of interdependence pertains to coordination and integration. If societies participating in this system want to preserve the free movement of goods, persons, and capital, as well as freedom to choose, while simultaneously avoiding mutual interference and disturbance of policies, they have but one course. They must coordinate their policies and develop instruments of control which will let them enjoy the advantages of effective national policies and an interdependent economic system.

Given the extent of interdependence today, which by far exceeds that of the 1920's and 1930's, failure to coordinate policies would be disastrous. The substantial and lasting economic recession which could result from disruption in the present international economic system might seriously threaten democracy in a number of countries. Moreover, such disruption, in the form of a breakdown of economic cooperation, reprisals, trade wars, or Bloc rivalries, could quickly erode the bases of cooperative security and hence threaten international stability.

Present economic strains between North America and Europe (and Japan) do not arise from calculated design but primarily as the natural consequence of the new highly interdependent international economy for which there is as yet no appropriate steering mechanism. These economic strains are all the more serious since they occur at a time when changing security relations in the Northern Hemisphere require a particular effort to maintain the cooperative basis of North America's and Europe's common security.

The American Illusion of Aloofness

America, Europe, and Japan have a considerable stake in fundamental reform of the international economic system leading to more effective management of economic interdependence. This necessity is reasonably well-recognized in Europe and Japan because of the special importance of foreign trade to both areas. But protectionist practices and a deep-rooted desire for national autonomy still form strong obstacles to the kinds of bold steps necessary to bridge the gap between recognition of the need for reform and actual measures to achieve it.

The situation is worse in the United States. Although there are many forces which see the necessity for reform and for an American contribution to the maintenance of a liberal system of interdependence, other forces advocating withdrawal from the international economic system of interdependence have visibly gained ground in recent years. In some of the external measures of August, 1971, the U.S. Executive Branch for the first time relinquished its traditional role as the defender of liberal trade practices. Moreover, protectionist sentiment is rising inside organized groups and within the Congress, partly in response to what are regarded as protectionist practices on the part of Europe and Japan. Thus, a vicious circle has been established with a momentum of its own. In addition, organized labor has joined these forces, on the ground that the export of capital by multinational corporations "exports American jobs" and that liberal trade practices threaten American employment.[1] But the employment argument against capital export is partially incorrect and protectionism to preserve jobs is a false alternative, as will be explained later.

Protectionist forces in the United States Congress and in wide sectors of the public assume that because of its

---

[1] See C. Fred Bergsten, "Crisis in U.S. Trade Policy," *Foreign Affairs,* July, 1971 (Vol. 49, No. 4), pp. 619-635.

low dependence on foreign trade, the United States can
afford partial withdrawal from its free trade practices of
the past and that it can, indeed, leave reorganization of
the international economic system to the outside world.

A comparison of the relative importance of foreign
trade—only 4% of the GNP in the United States as
opposed to 8% for the (enlarged) European Community
and 16% for Japan—suggests at first glance that the
United States may be able to afford a protectionist policy,
and that it can leave the job of reforming international
trade to others.

But a look at the future shows that the relevance of
foreign trade to the American economy is bound to change
quite drastically. At the moment, the United States is only
marginally dependent on petroleum imports, but, as a
result of a domestic decrease in production and constant
expansion of energy consumption, America will be dependent on imports for 50-60% by 1985—even taking into
account full-scale production in Alaska. This means that
the United States will import approximately $32 billion
worth of oil per year by 1985 and approximately $36
billion by 1990.[2]

The situation is similar with regard to minerals. In 1970
the United States was dependent on imports for more than
half of its supply of six minerals among the 13 most important minerals. By 1985, that percentage is projected for
nine minerals and, by the year 2000, for 12 out of the 13.[3]

---

[2] A MITRE Corporation estimate based on *The U.S. Energy Outlook,*
a Report by the National Petroleum Council, Vol. 1, July, 1971, p. 27.
The estimated price of $6 per barrel represents a relatively conservative
estimate and will in all likelihood be higher.

[3] Lester Brown, *Re-thinking the U.S. Relationship With the Rest of
the World,* a paper prepared for the Aspen Institute for Humanistic
Studies, Institute for National Alternatives Workshop, August, 1972.
For detailed computations see Nazli Choucri with James P. Bennett,
"Population, Resources and Technology: Political Implications of the
Environmental Crisis," in David A. Kay and Eugene B. Skolnikoff, eds.,
International Institutions and the Environmental Crisis, special issue,
International Organization, Spring 1972 (Vol. 26, No. 2), pp. 175-212.

In financial terms, this means that instead of spending approximately $8 billion (of its total imports of $40 billion) on energy fuels and minerals, as it did in 1970, the U.S. will spend $38 billion in 1985.

This drastic increase in U.S. dependence on imports (which is even greater than these figures suggest, owing to the relevance of these products for a highly-industrialized society) leads to two conclusions. First, the United States will need access to resources which will be possible only in a reasonably well-functioning system of international exchange and cooperation. Second, so that it may finance imports on the scale required in future, the United States has a vital stake in a liberalized world trading system in order to find markets for its exports, because they will have to be drastically larger than today.

In view of these realities, a policy of U.S. protectionism and neglect of urgently needed reform of the international economic system would be as short-sighted and self-defeating at home as it would be disastrous for the European Community or Japan. A policy of "benign neglect" amounts to a policy of self-neglect.

Strains with the European Community

The enlarged European Community is a grouping with remarkable wealth and power. Composed of nine European countries with a population of 253 million, the Community in 1970 had a GNP of $624 billion, *i.e.,* two-thirds that of the United States and considerably more than the Soviet GNP. In 1970, the Community's share of world trade (excluding trade among the members) was 25.5%, compared with 18.3% for the U.S. and 8.4% for Japan.[4]

This result represents an extraordinary success for common sense and hard work by European political

---

[4] *The European Community and the United States: 1972,* Study prepared by the Spokesman's Group of the Commission of the European Communities (Brussels, p. 27, June, 1972). Unless otherwise stated, the figures in this chapter are taken from this study. The percentage figures above still count Norway as a member.

leaders, who, in an arduous process over several decades, have succeeded in overcoming age-old national divisions and in forging this grouping amidst unprecedented prosperity in Europe. This new and powerful agglomeration also represents a great success for American policy for, without the Marshall Plan, its incentives for European unification, and constant American support, this grouping is unlikely to have emerged.

But American attitudes toward the European Community are changing. Many of the American leaders who were instrumental in building and supporting the Community no longer hold office. The number of active supporters of European unity among the American elite has dwindled considerably. Some disappointment with the slow process of unification and rising perception of the European Community as a competitor and rival explain this change. An increasing number of Americans are firmly convinced that Western Europe, Japan, and other countries unfairly discriminate against the United States and that her present monetary and trade problems are due mainly to outside discrimination. This belief is sharpened by resentment in light of past American generosity to Europe. Though such judgments are largely unfounded, they are a political reality and introduce an element of irrationality into European-American relations. Many Americans no longer endorse American support for European unity, once regarded as a wise and forward-looking policy in the enlightened self-interest of the United States. Some now even regard it as contrary to American interests.

To be sure, U.S. government policy has not ceased to support European unification. Advocating a "common ground in a consensus of independent policies" between Europe and America, President Nixon in his "State of the World" to Congress of February, 1972, stated, "This essential harmony of our purposes is the enduring link between a uniting Europe and the United States. This is why we have always favored European unity and why we welcome its growth not only in geographical area but also into new spheres of policy." But what the President identifies in the same message as "new developments" and "certain problems" are seen by certain sectors of Congressional opinion and the American public in more negative terms. They regard them as irritants, signs of disregard of American interest, selfishness, and an open challenge to the United States and the existing international order.

A brief analysis of the major problems in European-American relations will help us gain some insight, not only about the most abrasive factor in trans-Atlantic relations, but also about problems which are relevant to American and European relations with Japan and to the international economy and its reform in general.

Discrimination

In the past the United States accepted without question the discrimination against American goods which was inherent in formation of a customs union among the countries of the European Economic Community. It did so primarily for two reasons: First, it was hoped that the customs union would be a first step toward an economic union, to be followed by a political union. This was, in fact, the stated goal of the European states. Second, support of the Community occurred at a time when the strengthening of Western Europe through unification was considered particularly desirable in view of the East-West conflict in Europe.

But today the exigencies of the East-West conflict appear less stringent. Moreover, the hopes for European political union are dimmer. With enlargement of the Community to include Britain and two other European states— and no political union in sight—doubts have grown in the American public about the desirability of this process. In the absence of political unity, the new grouping appears to many Americans as a huge customs arrangement with an anachronistic agricultural policy which discriminates against American goods. Such views are mingled with perception of the Community as an economic bloc or rival, with Europeans, forgetful of what America did for them in the post-war period, seen as ganging up against American interests.

In light of increasingly emotional reactions toward the European Community, a sober look at the factual situation is urgently required.

If we look at the average tariffs on industrial products as computed in the Williams Report[5] and a study of the European Community,[6] the record of the Community compares quite favorably with the records of the United States, Japan, and the United Kingdom, as the following table illustrates.

Average Tariffs on Industrial Products

	Williams Report	EC Study
EEC (Six)	4.0%	6.0%
United States	6.1%	7.1%
Japan	5.7%	9.7%
United Kingdom	6.3%	7.6%

(NB. The differences are due to different methods of weighting.)

Although enlargement of the Community gives the Six free access to new markets, it should have a positive effect on outsiders since enlargement resulted not in a new average external tariff, but in maintenance of the old one. This means that the British tariff will sink to the level of the Community.

In terms of average percentages, Community tariffs are lower than those of the United States. But their protective character is even lower than these figures suggest because

---

[5] *United States International Economic Policy in an Interdependent World.* Report to the President submitted by the Commission on International Trade and Investment Policy (Williams Report), (Washington, D. C.: GPO, 1971).

[6] *The European Community and the United States: 1972, op. cit.*

of the averaging process used during formation of the external tariff. Thus, in post-Kennedy Round rates, only 13.1% of EEC tariffs on industrial goods are over 10% and only 2.4% are over 15%, whereas 38.3% of American tariffs are over 10% and 20.3% are over 15%.

With regard to quantitative restrictions, the picture is somewhat more balanced. In the United States the number of categories subject to quantitative restrictions when imported from OECD countries went up from 7 in 1963 to 67 in 1970 (not including some Japanese export restraints); in the European Community they decreased from 76 to 65 in the same period.

But the factor which matters most in attempting to judge the discriminatory effect of the European Community is the actual impact of its trade barriers on American exports. In point of fact, the formation of the European Community has provided a major boost to American exports. In 1958, the United States exported $2.8 billion to the Community (and imported $1.7 billion from it). By 1971, American exports had grown to $9.0 billion, and imports had risen to $7.7 billion.

In short, the European Community has had a continuous and major trade deficit with the United States, averaging $1.7 billion annually. In 1971, when the overall U.S. trade deficit was more than $2 billion, the Community was the only major industrialized area with which the United States had a trade surplus of $1.3 billion. If the past is any guide to the future, the enlargement of the Community should have a positive impact on American exports to Western Europe.

Though there are undoubtedly some problems in American-Community relations, including agriculture and non-tariff barriers, the European Community—far from being harmful to the United States—represents a major asset to American economic interests. Recognition of this fact in future debates would contribute greatly to a more rational approach.

Preferential Agreements

What most concerns official American spokesmen and
the informed public about the European Community (besides agriculture) are the various preferential agreements
linking the European Community to a host of European,
Mediterranean, and African countries. These agreements
differ considerably in their objectives and in their economic implications for the United States.

The European Free Trade Area

Since not all members of the former European Free
Trade Association (EFTA) were able to join Britain, Den-
mark, and Ireland in becoming members of the European
Community, a free-trade area according to GATT rules was
negotiated between the enlarged Community and Austria,
Finland, Sweden, Switzerland, Iceland, and Portugal. (Norway, after having rejected adhesion to the Community in
a plebiscite, will in all likelihood also apply for membership.) The free trade area, which enters into force in
January, 1973, will reduce all industrial tariffs, except for
13 items, among the 15 countries and 296 million people
of Western Europe (not counting Norway) until 1977.

It is natural that removal of internal barriers in this most
prosperous area of the globe outside the United States
raises questions in America about whether American exports in this region may be damaged. But for the European
states which could not join the European Community—
primarily for reasons of neutrality—there was no other
possible solution. As a result of a long history of economic
interaction, they were completely dependent on access to
this market. The following amount of their trade would
have been with the enlarged Community (including Norway whose membership was at that time assumed): Sweden
60%, Austria 50%, Finland 50%, Switzerland 50%, Portugal 45%, and Iceland 40%. In 1970 55% of Norway's
external trade was with the nine countries of the enlarged
Community; she had therefore no choice but to try to join

the free trade area. Conversely, the European Community simply could not have taken upon itself political responsibility for disrupting the external trade relations and internal economies of these countries so highly dependent on trade with the Community.

In 1970, the United States exported $1.3 billion to these six countries (3.5% of American exports). It is to be hoped that the trade-creating effects of the new grouping will increase American exports as was the case with the EEC. Nevertheless, the real answer lies in reducing the differential effect of the free-trade area by cutting tariffs.

The Preferential Agreements with Africa

Since its establishment, the Community has concluded association agreements with 18 African countries (including the Malagasy Republic). The agreements were concluded in the form of a free-trade area. Their purpose was to make the Community assume some of the responsibilities previously held by former colonial powers and to help the African states develop through trade and development aid. Since 1958, $2.2 billion have been granted to them. More recently, in the wake of Britain's joining the European Community, Kenya, Uganda, and Tanzania also concluded association agreements along similar lines. The Community intends, in the interest of equity, to conclude similar arrangements with other developing countries in comparable situations if they apply.

So far these agreements have had no negative effect on American trade. Between 1958 and 1971, American exports to the 18 African countries rose by 158%, as compared with 97% for the Community (although, for historical reasons, the latter's share remains, of course, significantly larger).

The Mediterranean Agreements

The Community has also conducted a number of association agreements with Greece, Turkey, Morocco, Spain,

Israel, and Malta which differ considerably both from each other and from the African agreements.

In the case of the European countries, Greece and Turkey, the agreements are designed to help them develop sufficiently to become full members of the Community, with participation in the customs union, institutions, etc. For this reason both countries receive aid from the Community and participate in reducing trade obstacles. So far these agreements have shown no discriminatory effect. American exports to both have continued to grow.

Behind the Greek and Turkish agreements there are, of course, important political motives. The Community shares a belief that these two European countries should be assisted in their development by the wealthier European countries and brought gradually into close association with the unification process of the European democracies. Both countries are of strategic importance to Western Europe, as well as to NATO, thus justifying a special effort towards association and integration. That these motives are shared by the United States at the political strategic level is shown by the bilateral security assistance she grants to these two countries.

Finally, the Community has concluded bilateral agreements with Morocco, Spain, Israel, and Malta. While the agreements with Morocco and Malta gradually establish free trade areas and, consequently, fulfill GATT rules, it has been argued that the agreements with Spain and Israel violate GATT provisions. Here again, however, the case should not be judged without taking into consideration political strategic motives. The Community is interested in gradually reintegrating Spain into the system of democratic states north of her borders. To achieve this, the Community must both encourage internal change and strengthen Spain's links with the area to which she naturally belongs.

The case of Israel is somewhat different. The European Community cannot remain indifferent to the fate of Israel within a hostile environment; it desires the survival of

Israel through an equitable peace in the Middle East. It is to strengthen Israel, which is highly dependent on trade with the outside world, that the Community has concluded its commercial treaty.

In the case of both Spain and Israel, the political and strategic objectives of the United States and Europe are basically alike. Moreover the advantages granted to these countries through EEC arrangements amount to less—indeed, only a fraction in the case of Israel—than the special assistance which both states receive from the United States.

In conclusion, it must be said that the total Mediterranean area, excluding Italy and France, accounts for only 6% of U.S. exports and 3% of imports. So far, Community arrangements in the Mediterranean have had no negative impact on American exports. But in order to meet American concerns, the Community, first unilaterally and then later in bilateral negotiations with the United States, lowered its tariff on citrus fruit from America by between 30 and 60% as a means of reducing the preferential treatment given to Mediterranean countries. In November, 1972 the Council of Ministers of the Community considered for the first time the possibility of a Mediterranean policy which attempts to harmonize the disparate arrangements.

The agreements with the Mediterranean and African countries do, however, raise a more fundamental question which the Community and the associated states must face in the near future: Is it desirable that, for historical reasons, one group of developing countries has preferential access to a highly industrialized area while other developing countries are treated less favorably? This unequal treatment of different areas of the Third World could result in other attempts to establish equally privileged access to other industrialized areas, *e.g.,* for the Latin American countries vis-à-vis the United States. The emergence of preferential arrangements which would reorder North-

South relationships on a regional basis is not a desirable solution.

Agriculture

Of all problems in European-American relations the agricultural question is probably the source of greatest concern in the United States. The Common Agricultural Policy (CAP) is regarded as a highly protectionist device which seriously harms the possibilities of American agricultural exports to the Community. In the words of the Williams Report, "The implementation of the Common Agricultural Policy by the European Community was the principal obstacle during the decade (of the 1960's) to lowering agricultural trade barriers, although it was by no means the only one." [7]

On both sides of the Atlantic, agriculture represents a sector where the standard of living and modernization have lagged behind other sectors of society. The farm vote is politically over-represented on both sides of the Atlantic. It is more important in Europe, where 13% of the working population is employed in agriculture, than it is in the United States, where farm workers constitute 4.5% of the labor force. As a result, governments on both sides have developed a complex system of support, subsidies, and protection in order to raise farm income.

The European Community assures agricultural income through a system of guaranteed prices and variable levies for a number of commodities that enter the Community. This system offers complete protection for a number of items such as wheat or milk products. (But some products, such as soy beans from the United States, which accounted for nearly $800 million in 1971, enter the Community duty free.) As a result of the CAP, European consumers pay prices up to several times higher than the world market price.

A particularly irritating consequence of the CAP to the United States and other exporters of agriculture relates

---

[7] *Williams Report, op. cit.,* p. 143.

to the disposal of over-production encouraged by high European prices. Excess agricultural production is sold by the Community on the world market with high subsidies—totalling $1 billion 1968-69—in competition with other countries' products. The United States also subsidizes agricultural exports (*e.g.*, the 1972 grain sale to the USSR), but the total amount of U.S. support is much lower.

American government support for agriculture combines direct income support for farms with quantitative import restrictions on many agricultural products, as well as subsidies to keep down production and promote exports of surplus products. As a result of the 1955 waiver to the GATT rules, roughly one-half of American agricultural production is shielded by quantitative restrictions. The mechanism of mutual protection is demonstrated by the case of butter. The Community's variable levy on butter in 1969 was higher than 300%, as compared with the American duty of 10-15%, but the U.S. butter import quota was so low that it practically prohibited any imports.

The costs of this system to the European consumer are enormous. According to one estimate, the total cost of the Common Agricultural Policy is somewhere between $11-13 billion yearly.[8] But the cost of income support for agricultural workers in America is not small either. According to an independent study, the European Community supports each agricultural worker by some $860 annually and the United States by $1,320.[9]

As a result of the CAP, American exports of agricultural products subject to the levy system dropped by about half, to $0.4 billion in 1970. Nevertheless, American agricultural exports as a whole expanded as a result of

---

[8] "A Future for European Agriculture," *The Atlantic Papers,* No. 4 (Paris: The Atlantic Institute, 1970), p. 9.

[9] "Comparaison entre le soutien accordé à l'agriculture aux Etats-Unis et dans la Communauté," by G. Vandewalle and W. Meeusen, 1971 quoted in *The European Community and the United States: 1972, op. cit.,* p. 3.

the spectacular sales increase of specific products. American agricultural exports to the Community rose from $1.2 billion in 1964, the last trade year prior to the beginning of the CAP, to $1.7 billion in 1971—compared with Community agricultural exports to the U.S. of $423 million—thus creating an agricultural trade surplus of $1.3 billion in favor of the United States.

While both Europeans and Americans might rightly complain about the protectionist character of these agricultural support systems, the fact that American agricultural exports to the Community increased by 42% over the last seven years, while increasing only 26% to the rest of the world, shows that American agriculture did not do so badly in Europe as is sometimes suggested in public statements. In fact, the agricultural surplus to the Community accounts for a large part of the trade surplus that America enjoys with the Community.

Needless to say, the problem does not end here. America's surplus is achieved primarily through a few products. What concerns Americans most is the denial of a *potential* increase in agricultural exports to the Community. Although the CAP merely replaced various, equally effective national systems of agricultural protection by one unified system, Americans were disappointed at the Community's unwillingness to open its agricultural market to the outside world. If there were a genuinely free market in agricultural products, the United States, with its more efficient methods of production, its climate, and good soil, would fare much better with most products than would the Europeans.

In theory, a shift of production to the location of its lowest cost would result in a considerable decrease in food prices for the European consumer and would therefore be desirable. But as Americans themselves know, the political and social problem of helping the farm population—which in some regions of Europe, particularly Southern Italy, reaches up to 50%—adapt to modernization must not be underestimated. Any future attempt to reduce agricultural protectionism will have to face this particular issue.

Distortions of International Competition

The United States, Europe, and Japan have a long-lasting tradition of various practices which distort international competition. These measures may differ in ingenuity, sector, character, or effectiveness, but none of these countries can accuse the other of such practices without also accusing itself.

Among the practices are a variety of non-tariff barriers, particularly "voluntary" restraints on imports; certain valuation practices, particularly the "American selling price system"; certain taxes that may affect foreign trade; administrative obstacles, in the form of certain standards relating to health, pollution, hygiene, etc.; government procurement practices such as the "Buy American Act" or administrative discretion as practiced by public authorities in Europe; anti-dumping and countervailing duties; and export subsidies.

American Investment in Europe and Multinational Corporations

American investment in Europe is of growing importance in Atlantic economic relations, but the problems it raises far transcend relations between the United States and Europe.

By 1970 the book value of direct American investment in the Community of the Six was $11.7 billion, having risen from $1.9 billion in 1958, not including investments by American holding companies in such places as Switzerland or the Bahamas. This investment represented 15% of all American investments abroad. Because of the special importance of Britain as a location for American investment, enlargement of the Community has almost doubled American investment in the Community, to a book value of $20.5 billion.

How important these investments have become in
Europe and to European-American economic relations is
demonstrated by two figures. In 1968, American manu-
facturing subsidiaries within the Community sold $14
billion worth of goods (compared with $4.8 billion in
1961); in 1971 they repatriated $1.2 billion, from profits
made within the Community, re-investing the remaining
profits in Europe.

By contrast, direct investment by the six Community
countries in the United States is considerably lower. Its
book value was only $3.5 billion in 1970 (although direct
investment from Europe as a whole amounts to approximately $9 billion).[10]

American companies have made extraordinary use of
the opportunities offered by the huge European market
created by the European Community. From the beginning
their investment and planning of production and research
took the vast market as a frame of action, something which
the European companies have been very reluctant to do,
clinging on the whole to their traditional national markets
and preferring instead arrangements with national companies in other parts of the Community. As Servan-
Schreiber rightly noted in *The American Challenge,* the
only truly European companies are American.

Conversely, the absence of direct European investment
in America can be partially explained by an unfavorable
U.S. climate for foreign investment. Foreign investment is
simply not allowed in many U.S. industries, *e.g.,* in avia-
tion, insurance, or the manufacture of some beverages.
Moreover, American anti-trust laws are enforced not only
against American subsidiaries of foreign firms but also
against the parent companies for business they conduct
outside the United States—a practice not to be found
within the Community, which applies its anti-trust laws

---

[10] Jack N. Behrman, "New Orientation in International Trade and
Investment," in: Pierre Uri, ed., *Trade and Investment Policies for the
Seventies. New Challenges for the Atlantic Area and Japan* (New York:
Praeger Publishers, 1971), p. 13.

only to activities within Europe. Beginning an investment by acquiring an existing firm, a common American practice in Europe, often meets strong American administrative resistance.

In addition to inequality of investment opportunities, a second problem arising from American investment in Europe leads to differing views between Americans and Europeans on an important issue. Americans have a tendency to blame two factors for the U.S. balance of payments deficit of recent years: Weak American export performance owing in part to protectionism abroad, and U.S. military costs abroad. As a result they demand that their European partners create better access for American goods and contribute more generously to American military expenditures.

Europeans view this problem rather differently. They point out that the U.S. trade deficit of $2 billion in 1971 was only a small fraction of the deficit in official reserve transactions, amounting to $29.8 billion, in the same year. Moreover, the Community was the only area where the United States achieved a trade surplus. Nor does the military cost to the balance of payments deficit of around $1.2 billion annually seem a major factor to Europeans. In their opinion what really caused the large deficit was the huge movements of U.S. capital, including $4.5 billion for foreign investments in 1971.

Despite technological and economic advantages derived from American investment, many Europeans regard the growth of such investment, resulting in huge unproductive dollar and gold holdings, as an important question to be dealt with in trying to resolve U.S.-European imbalances over the long term—perhaps equal in importance to trade, where Europeans feel that they are treating the United States no worse than America is treating them.

The problem of investment raises fundamental questions for all industrialized and developing countries. The rise of the multinational corporation and of "international production" by companies in other countries is likely radically to change international economic relations and the manner in which governments insure their functioning.

According to one estimate, total sales of all multinational corporations in the world in 1970 amounted to $450 billion as compared with total world exports of $300 billion.[11] U.S.-owned corporations had an international production of $219 billion, compared with American merchandise exports of $40 billion in that year.

Present trends in international investment and production, as well as in domestic production, point to a profound change in the international economy. Since international production has consistently risen by about 10% per year, while the total GNP growth of the non-Communist world has stayed around 4% annually, international production seems likely to rise from its present 22% of total production in the non-Communist world to 35% by 1980 and 50% by 1990.

In a world in which a substantial share of the production is planned and managed by international companies, present concepts of comparative advantage and of insuring free trade may be inadequate and obsolete. Investment decisions on a large scale will increasingly be based not on comparative advantage but on non-trade considerations such as general economic environment or policies of the host government.

Since even today 30% of total U.S. foreign trade is intra-company trade, *i.e.,* goods exchanged between national subsidiaries of the same parent company, we arrive at a startling conclusion. The future of international trade will to an increasing extent depend not so much on the classical instruments for liberalizing trade *but on the manner in which large corporations conduct their internal business and in the ways in which governments influence them.* This state of affairs calls for an entirely new approach and a new set of rules. New rules are all

---

[11] Jack N. Behrman, "New Orientation in International Trade and Investment," *op. cit.*

the more needed since multinational corporations also raise problems for their host countries either by acquiring political influence which is judged too dominant or, in some cases, by counteracting national policies through internal decisions on investments or profit allocation.

In recent years, American and other trade unions have become increasingly opposed to multinational corporations. They have objected mainly to the export of capital which, in their opinion, removes jobs from the parent company. Because of labor's political and economic importance on both sides of the Atlantic, rational discussion of this issue with the trade unions would seem particularly important.

Although it is exceedingly difficult to assess the precise impact of international investment on trade and employment, objections to international investment on the grounds of job exportation seem to be questionable. First, foreign investment is not a one-way street. Investment by outsiders also creates employment in the United States. Thus, while American-owned international production in 1970 amounted to $219 billion, production in the United States owned by foreign portfolio investors and foreign direct investors totalled a respectable $100 billion.[12]

Second, a large part of American investment abroad *cannot* export jobs since it involves production, such as oil or raw materials production, which cannot be carried out domestically. Finally, foreign investments are made for many reasons other than the prospect of obtaining cheaper labor, including a desire to avoid high transportation costs, the advantages of being behind trade barriers, location close to the consumer, etc.

If this production is lost at home, it would have been lost anyhow, since industries of other countries will sooner or later use these investment opportunities. Moreover, labor leaders often overlook the fact that U.S. companies

---

[12] Behrman, *op. cit.*, p. 13.

operating abroad support employment at home through purchases from their parent company.

Labor's growing concern over foreign investments, combined in the United States with increasingly protectionist attitudes, does, however, point to an important problem: In all our societies, there is growing consensus that social justice requires protection of the individual against hardships, such as loss of work or income, arising from economic change. As economic interdependence grows, conflicts between social justice and competition are less apt to arise within the national framework, where they can be resolved by intervention of the political authority, than in the international context, where there is no superior authority to resolve competing claims at national and multinational levels. Thus, our earlier conclusion that the emerging multinational system of economic interdependence requires new mechanisms for coordination of national policies applies to this area as well.

It is obvious that multinational corporations and international production have both advantages and disadvantages. They constitute an increasingly important element of the emerging multinational economy of interdependence. What is needed is not to eliminate them but to regulate them in a way which will insure their positive contribution.

The Inadequacy of the International Monetary System

The crisis of the international monetary system is undoubtedly the most serious aspect of the present critical phase of the international economy. If this system cannot be reformed and put in order within the next few years, all other reform measures in the field of trade or international investment are likely to be futile. The international economic system is likely to be disrupted with far-reaching implications for political cooperation and security in the West.

Although the monetary system that was created at Bretton Woods is in crisis today, it served its purpose remarkably well for almost a quarter of a century. Despite its shortcomings, it provided the monetary foundation for an upsurge of international trade and world production unequalled in history in addition to accommodating the rise of West Germany and Japan—enemy countries at the time of Bretton Woods—as well as many newly independent states. Considering the strains inevitably caused by such developments, it is remarkable that the system lasted as long as it did.

While various post-war incidents exposed serious weaknesses, it was only in the late 1960's that the basic inadequacy of the system became obvious. The American measures of August, 1971, and the Smithsonian Agreement of December, 1971, put an end to basic features of the old system and, along with the imposition of foreign exchange controls in France and Germany, dramatically underscored the need for major reform.

The Bretton Woods system has become inadequate because neither its adjustment mechanisms nor its system of providing liquidity and reserves correspond to the needs of the contemporary economic system. When the adjustment mechanism was discussed at Bretton Woods, both the Keynes Plan and the White Plan had provisions for a supranational authority which could influence decisions regarding modification of the exchange rates when a country could no longer balance its accounts with the outside world.[13] Indeed, a provision was discussed which would have imposed interest on the holdings of a country with a surplus.

But neither a supra-national authority nor stringent rules on adjustment was accepted at Bretton Woods. The ultimate decision on adjusting exchange rates was left to national discretion. This arrangement created one of

---

[13] The discussions of those years continue to be highly relevant today. For an admirable analysis brought up to date, see: Richard N. Gardner, *Sterling-Dollar Diplomacy. The Origins and the Prospect of our International Economic Order,* rev. ed. (New York: McGraw-Hill Book Co., 1969).

the main problems of the Bretton Woods system. Deficit countries tended to postpone adjustment for internal political and economic reasons, until circumstances became highly critical. Surplus countries had no incentive to adjust exchange rates in time and revalued only under speculative pressure in a crisis when it was too late for moderate action.

The system, therefore, badly needs an adjustment mechanism which is not so excessively flexible as to undermine certainty and economic predictability and yet is flexible enough to avoid shock wave adjustments which rock attempts at economic and political cooperation as has been the case in the past.

The second inadequacy of the present monetary system lies in its mechanisms for providing liquidity and reserves. Thirty years ago Keynes suggested creating a clearing union with a man-made reserve unit and relatively unlimited credit facilities for every country. This plan was not accepted, primarily because of resistance by the United States, which then assumed that it would remain a surplus country and objected on the grounds that such a system would make it too easy for others and would place a permanent burden on America. The system which was finally adopted followed the American concept in the main. It provided dollars for a central fund and tied up credit facilities with considerable restrictions, so that the United States was unable to use the system. Gold became a means for international settlement.

World gold production was, however, unable to keep pace with the extraordinary expansion of world trade. Similarly, the International Monetary Fund was unable to provide funds to finance the growth of world trade because of its limited reserves and the restrictions on credit. Dollars were used for that purpose. As a result the world gradually slipped into a dollar standard, the necessary liquidity being created by a deficit in the American balance of payments. Other countries were quite willing to go along with this system, accepting either gold from the

American reserves or dollars from the American printing press.

But this state of affairs became increasingly unacceptable as the American gold supply dwindled and the dollar holdings of foreign central banks rose to an unprecedented $51 billion in 1971. When President Nixon in August, 1971, suspended the dollar's convertibility into gold, two things had become obvious. Despite the economic strength of the United States, the dollar alone could no longer play the role of the main reserve currency for the world monetary system. Second, the independence enjoyed by the United States as a result of that role no longer appeared acceptable. With large amounts of short- and long-term capital leaving the United States for profitable use elsewhere, other countries had no choice but to accept unproductive dollars, which they already possessed in considerable amounts, thus worsening their problems of domestic inflation. In the absence of substantial realignments of exchange rates, the growing trade deficit of the United States and its military expenditures overseas further aggravated the problem. Finally, the system placed the burden of adjustment on other currencies, a task which was most difficult since an adjustment aimed at the dollar automatically also affected a currency's position *vis à vis* all other currencies.

Approaches to the Future

The conviction is growing in all Western countries that basic change in the international economic system is urgently needed but governments are only beginning to sketch the first outlines of possible reforms. First steps were made with the U.S. Government's proposal for monetary reform of September 26, 1972, and the declaration by the heads of governments of the European Community on October 20, 1972. Debate on these issues is gaining momentum among experts and reveals remarkable consensus on a number of general principles. In addition to a growing number of individual contributions, some groups have also made attempts to view all these problems in an integrated perspective: examples include the report of the President's Commission on International Trade and Investment Policy of 1971 already quoted; a report by American, European, and Japanese economists;[14] and, most recently, an Interim Report by the Monetary Committee of the Atlantic Council of the United States.[15] These reports contain a number of fruitful suggestions.

In approaching the future, governments must bear in mind that, as in the nuclear world of security policy, the international interdependence of the economic sphere renders obsolete the classical concepts of state behavior. There will be no complete national autonomy nor national gains at the expense of others' losses, but only a world-wide community of winners or losers.

A Reform of the International Monetary System

The Smithsonian Agreement of December, 1971, drew some obvious conclusions from the situation created by the measures of the American government in August, 1971.

The revaluation of the main currencies *vis à vis* the U.S. dollar, the devaluation of the dollar, the widening of the margin of fluctuation for currencies and, finally, the removal of the 10% surcharge by the United States eliminated the most urgent international monetary problems.

---

[14] "Dreiparteienbericht ueber eine Neugestaltung der internationalen Waehrungsordnung," *Europe Dokumente*, No. 658-659 (Luxembourg: Europe. Agence Internationale d'Information pour la Presse, 7 January, 1972).

[15] *To Modernize the International Monetary System*, interim report of the Monetary Committee of the Atlantic Council of the United States, September 18, 1972, mimeographed. See also Richard N. Gardner, "Toward a New 'Bretton Woods.' The Politics of International Monetary Reform," *The Banker*, September, 1972, p. 1136-1138; and in particular Robert Triffin, *Basic Considerations on International Monetary Reform*, mimeographed, November, 1972, and *Prospects for International Monetary Reform*, mimeographed, December, 1972.

These measures helped to avert a worse crisis, but the long-term problems now demand attention.

The Adjustment Problem

There are three approaches to long-term solutions to the adjustment problem.

The best approach to adjustment is, of course, to make it unnecessary or infrequent. To be sure, as long as there are autonomous nations with differing priorities, economic policies, and economic starting points, the likelihood of imbalances in their relationships with each other will exist always. But the rewards of interdependence multiply if states can succeed in coordinating their economic policies.

Most important in this connection would be a concerted effort to slow down the speculative movements of short-term capital which have in the past triggered so many crises (though usually reflecting and accelerating a pre-existing structural imbalance). Coordination of interest rates, of conditions on the placement of short-term capital, or of taxes could have considerable impact. But coordination to avoid imbalances between countries can, of course, go much further, covering practically all fields of economic policy.

During the coming discussions on reform in this field, states will have to face a choice which was discussed much earlier both at Bretton Woods and in connection with the Charter of the International Trade Organization: Either states submit to rules of economic behavior and coordination and accept advice, if not decisions, by international organizations or, owing to the high degree of interaction among their economies which tends to accentuate imbalances, they will have to live with the constant necessity for adjustment, with all its accompanying economic disadvantages.

The second approach to the problem is to create a better adjustment mechanism. The two main weaknesses of the present system are national discretion over the changes of parities of currencies, and fixed exchange rates, which can be changed only under disruptive conditions of crisis.

There is growing international consensus on the following elements of reform:

• Strong fluctuations in exchange rates are undesirable because they enhance economic uncertainty and unpredictability for individuals and governments alike. But a mechanism is needed which makes parity changes possible in small and frequent increments under commonly agreed conditions that require such adjustments from both surplus and deficit countries. (The currencies of the European Community would be submitted to a different rule since they will be increasingly tied together by reductions of the margins between them until a European Monetary Union, with a common currency, eventually emerges.)

The conditions and rules for such adjustments are, of course, a crucial element. They should not only stipulate that international organization must play an important role in bringing about adjustment, but also be sufficiently automatic, without being completely mechanistic, to press both deficit and surplus countries to adjust in cases of structural imbalance. Obviously, one must carefully define the conditions and indicators of imbalance and make sure that changes of exchange rates do not become a substitute for domestic employment policy.

It should be possible for international organizations to ask both deficit and surplus countries to make adjustments in their exchange rate, or specific changes in their domestic and external policies, or both. In case of noncompliance and serious repercussions in the international economy, it should be possible to apply sanctions either in the form of general surcharges or selective duties against a surplus country or by withholding credit facilities from deficit countries.

Finally, interim arrangements will be necesary, since it will take several years until international monetary reform can be worked out and implemented. It would be useful if dollars could be accepted without qualification and if the United States could assure against possible losses from a future increase in dollars as a result of devaluation. Moreover, the United States should cooperate with other countries in maintaining convertibility and stable exchange rates. The July, 1972, intervention of the United States was an encouraging step in that direction.

The Problem of Liquidity and Reserves

The second most important element in monetary reform is the creation of a new system of liquidity and reserves. There seems to be a growing consensus on the necessity for the following elements in such a system:

At the center, as the main reserve in lieu of dollars, should be Reserve Accounts with the International Monetary Fund, similar to the Special Drawing Rights (SDR's) of the past, but drastically expanded and adapted to the needs of the new system. The Reserve Accounts would be administered by the IMF and would be available to all countries under fixed conditions which would ensure that deficit countries comply with the general rules.

The annual expansion of international reserves would no longer be determined by the countries with key currencies, or by gold production, but by a decision-making process within IMF relating the expansion of reserves to the state of the gobal economy, international trade, and requirements of under-developed countries. These decisions should be based on the best advice available.

The new system should insure a return of the dollar to convertibility. This could be achieved by consolidating present large claims on main currencies, including the Pound Sterling. The holdings of central banks in such currencies could be deposited at the IMF and exchanged against SDR's. The IMF could then transform these dollar amounts into long-term liabilities of the United States (with a higher interest rate than the deposits) which America could gradually decrease. It is doubtful that it is politically feasible or economically possible without disruption to eliminate gold entirely from this system. While the SDRs would not be based on gold, gold should not entirely lose a role in settling international accounts; rather, it should be gradually phased out of the system through some process, for example, like the one proposed by Robert Triffin. [16]

The effectiveness of a new reserve system will depend entirely on confidence in its ability to work. A reserve currency is not created or abolished by the unilateral decision of a country holding it, but by the role it plays and by the confidence it inspires among other countries and private individuals. Thus, even with a new system centered on SDR's, it is highly likely that, owing to the economic position of the United States, the dollar will continue as a reserve currency, along with some other main currencies such as the Pound Sterling, the Mark, the Yen, and a common European currency.

The proposed elements of a new international monetary system would not impair creation of a common European currency. Within the Community, the harmonization of economic policy is obviously more important as an instrument of adjustment than the flexibility of exchange rates. Consequently, it will be necessary at an early stage both to tie the European currencies together through a common policy of intervention by their central banks, and assure that the process of coordinating economic policies becomes increasingly effective. Further steps in this direction were made at the European Summit Conference in October, 1972, notably through the establishment of a European Monetary Cooperation Fund.[17]

---

[16] Robert Triffin, *Prospects for International Monetary Reform, op. cit.,* p. 6f.

[17] On these problems see Robert Triffin, *Report on the First Phases of a European Monetary Cooperation Fund,* mimeographed, November, 1972.

If the preceding reforms are to be implemented, the IMF must be strengthened. If the present system of national autonomy is to be replaced by a multinational system for monetary management, the IMF will need stronger powers to advise and guide member countries and to impose sanctions in extreme cases. Equally important, the IMF would have to take on a new function as a forum for policy coordination. This would require more permanent mechanisms for consultation; representation of countries at the highest policy-making level, such as Central Bank Presidents or Finance Ministers; and more frequent IMF meetings.

In reviewing solutions for monetary reform, states should not forget a simple but important lesson: At Bretton Woods many states, notably the United States, started from the mistaken assumption that they would always remain in the economic position they held at that moment; this has been proven false. Surplus countries can quickly become deficit countries and vice versa. Only solutions which look at the system as a whole will serve the interests of all, whatever their monetary position may be today.

In addition to strengthening the IMF, it is desirable to assure more adequate representation in it by underdeveloped countries as a means of achieving greater harmony between international monetary and development policy. Adequate participation by these countries in decision-making and limited use of SDR's for development purposes should be attempted, although these issues are likely to create considerable controversy.

Participation in the discussions of reform or in the operation of the system at an early stage by Socialist countries, unless confined to one or two of the smaller states, would raise very complex problems. The questions to be solved are difficult enough. They would be further complicated by including countries with fundamentally different economic systems. New monetary arrangements with the Socialist world will become necessary as economic interaction grows, but it would probably be wise to postpone such negotiations until after the market economy countries have reached basic agreement among themselves. Until then, discussions might be carried out with Socialist countries in the form of parallel talks.

The Preservation and Establishment of Liberal Trade Practices
The Need for European Unity

The key to many American attitudes and to the preservation of cooperative ventures in many fields lies in Europe. Although the European Community has achieved remarkable success in establishing an internal common market, the future of true economic union, of a common foreign policy and defense, and of democratically established institutions remains uncertain. Mystical or narrow-minded nationalism continues to block the path toward political unity which had been the declared goal of former European and American political leaders. As a former American representative to the European Community put it, "At the moment of crisis, the absence of a European consensus necessarily leaves the United States with a feeling of confusion and malaise." [18]

As long as political unification of Western Europe (to be attained by passing through an intermediary stage of common economic policies) appeared to have a reasonable chance of success, there was general willingness in the United States to accept such economic measures as formation of a common market or preferential agreements on the grounds that these were necessary byproducts of political unification. But as long as it seems unlikely that the European Community will move beyond a customs union with agricultural protection and a system of preferential agreements with other states, Americans increasingly view the Community as an economic bloc

---

[18] J. Robert Schaetzel, "Die neuen Dimensionen der Beziehungen zwischen einer erweiterten Europäischen Gemeinschaft und den Vereinigten Staaten," *Europa—Archiv* (1971, No. 24), p. 860-1.

harmful to U.S. economic interests. It is thus under-
standable that American attitudes toward the Community
are no longer characterized by the enthusiastic support
of the early post-war years and have instead become
increasingly reserved.

The European Community absolutely must, therefore,
establish a European identity, common institutions, and
common policies in all fields of its activities, from monetary
affairs to trade, if a cooperative atmosphere between
America and Europe is to be preserved and if the international economic system is to be reformed in mutually
advantageous ways. One must agree with an American
observer who points to "the difficulty the European leaders
create for themselves and for the kind of understanding
they need elsewhere in the world by their own current
confusion (or timidity, or both) about what it is they are
seeking to build in Europe. A good, sharp dose of old-
fashioned European enthusiasm would do much to clear
the air." [19]

Monetary Reform and Free Trade

The replacement of distorted exchange rates by more
realistic ones and the introduction of more effective
adjustment mechanisms are likely significantly to affect
international trade and to offer new opportunities for an
undistorted international division of labor.[20] Monetary
reform will require modifications of internal production,
based today on the distorted exchange rates of the past.
The surplus countries especially, including Japan and
to a lesser extent West Germany, will be forced to create
additional domestic demand.

---

[19] Miriam Camps, *Sources of Strain in the Trans-Atlantic Relationship:
Strains Arising Primarily From American Politics and Attitudes,* Discussion paper for a European-American Conference at Royaumont, May 4-7,
1972, mimeographed, p. 17.

[20] We follow for this section the findings of, "Dreiparteienbericht
ueber eine Neugestaltung der internationalen Waehrungsordnung," *op.
cit.,* p. 7.

At the same time, elimination of the over-valuation of the dollar, which had contributed to the weak performance of American goods abroad, and, hopefully, reversal of the rising tide of protectionism in the United States should improve conditions for liberal practices in international trade.

At the present time many barriers and distortions in America, Japan, and Western Europe obstruct free trade. Some of these owe their existence to monetary difficulties. With the establishment of more realistic exchange rates and more adequate adjustment mechanisms which offer better opportunities for equilibrium among national balances of payments, the chances should improve for removing obstacles to trade.

Removing Tariffs and Quantitative Restrictions

After the Kennedy Round of tariff negotiations, average tariffs on industrialized goods in Western countries dropped to a level of 5-11%. This does not mean, however, that tariffs have become unimportant. On the contrary, the tariff structure continues to be selectively protectionist since there are still tariffs over 15% on many goods, and tariffs on some exceed 50%.

It is time to renew efforts aimed at liberalizing trade. The last set of negotiations during the Kennedy Round, characterized by a new negotiating style, greatly facilitated liberalization. But even more flexible negotiating procedures and a much more ambitious goal—agreement on complete elimination of all remaining tariffs within 10 years—should be adopted for the next GATT Round scheduled to begin in 1973.

Exceptions for industries which require prolonged transitional protection should not be achieved through continuation of tariffs but rather through internationally negotiated agreements on domestic adjustments and aids. In today's world the elimination of all tariffs could become meaningless since governments can now employ a wide range of other protectionist instruments, including subsidies and other means of support. But acceptance of the principles of elimination of all trade barriers and of achieving exceptions through international negotiations would constitute net progress since it would assure that needed exceptions to the free trade rule be subject to generally accepted standards and common review.

A complete reduction of all tariffs on industrial goods would eliminate the preferential treatment which the European Community now accords to European states in the European free trade area and to European and African states in association agreements. Moreover, some of the thorny issues in European-American trade relations, including the "American Selling Price" system and other questionable tariff valuation procedures on both sides of the Atlantic, would disappear since tariff valuation problems would go out with tariffs.

Except in Japan, quantitative restrictions had been generally eliminated by the late 1960's, as a result of many years of hard work. But in the more recent past they have made a comeback in the form of "voluntary" restraints negotiated between specific industries—usually under discreet, but effective, threat of governmental legislative action unless such restraints were put into effect.

"Voluntary" restraints are basically irreconcilable with a system of free trade. Although their defenders argue that they represent an instrument for controlling international trade which is much more flexible and easier to remove than quantitative restrictions or tariffs which require legislative action, they do, in fact, constitute a cartel mechanism which distorts competition.

Since these "voluntary" restraints appear to be growing in importance, it is time for the industrialized countries to decide whether they want to maintain and possibly expand an instrument of protection that is not subject to established procedures of international law and reflects not commonly established rules but the power relationships between the negotiating parties.

"Voluntary" restraints raise one basic question which has been mentioned in other contexts. There is need for some mechanism which will help backward or stagnant industries adapt to competition or to be phased out. Given the demands of social justice, such assistance should be given, but it must be based on commonly accepted standards if we are to achieve an equitable world trade system.

Preferential Agreements

As we explained earlier, the various preferential agreements through which the European Community has associated a number of European and African countries with its common market are of special concern not only to the United States. The size of the total preferential area created by these agreements inevitably undermines the validity of the Most Favored Nation treatment, a basic element of a liberal world trade system. The exceptions from the Most Favored National treatment permitted in the GATT rules were intended to cover special cases and not such a large area of the world.

If the industrialized countries could negotiate a universal reduction of tariffs on all industrial goods, the problem of preferential treatment would be largely eliminated. But in this instance some arrangement covering agricultural products and the transitional period until tariffs are removed completely would still be necessary.

As a first step, the European Community should begin to negotiate compensations to outsiders for possible trade diversions created by existing preferential agreements. (Under the GATT rules, third countries are entitled to such compensation but the Community has so far refused to negotiate although it has little to fear since the negative impact of the preferential agreements on trade with third countries appears to be negligible.) Second, the European Community, the United States, and Japan should review the Community's existing preferential agreements to assess their strategic desirability as well as their implications for an overall strategy on development aid. The three could then consider which industrial products warrant reduced preferences until such time as tariffs are eliminated completely, as well as suitable arrangements regarding agricultural products.

Agriculture

From an economic point of view of all the world's resources, agricultural resources are used least rationally. High-cost agricultural production in Western Europe is maintained at a cost of many billions a year while countries with low-cost agricultural production, including the United States and New Zealand, must restrict their own output. But political and social objectives rather than economic rationality prevail in almost all countries, especially in the European Community and Japan where a significant segment of the working population is still employed in agriculture.

Because of the economic hardships which would be created by complete liberalization of agricultural trade, it is unrealistic to expect a drastic change in official policy in Western Europe or Japan in the near future. Nevertheless, certain forces of economic change are at work which will improve the chances for liberalization.

In both Japan and the European Community, the percentage of agricultural workers in the active population has been declining constantly. In Japan it dropped from 40% in 1955 to 17% in 1970; within the European Community it declined from 21% in 1955 to 13% in 1970, with a projected decrease to 6% by 1980. Within the Community, the "Mansholt Plan" provides incentives for reducing farm population and increasing the competitiveness of farms by encouraging the formation of larger farms and by paying stipends to agricultural workers who leave the land.

These trends improve the conditions for effecting important changes needed in the agricultural support system and international trade. Within the Community the present system is not characterized by any special degree of social justice. Price supports benefit large and efficient farms which need such support far less than smaller farms. Moreover, the cost of this system to the consumer is enormous since he must pay not only prices which are way above world market levels but also the high costs of administering, storing, and discharging surpluses.

Once the farm population in the Community has decreased further, a system of direct income support to farmers would be an infinitely more rational and less costly means of supporting European agriculture.

Direct income support not only would be socially more just, since it would aid those who really need it, but also would enable the international market mechanism again to come into play in agriculture. The European Community, the United States, Japan, and such agricultural producers as New Zealand and Australia would have to draw up an agreement on conditions and amounts of farm support. The complicated system of protection involving variable levels, duties, or quotas now in use could then be discarded.

Meanwhile, some intermediate measures to liberalize agricultural trade are needed. Not only the European Community and Japan, but the United States, indulge in various forms of agricultural protection. In the interests of their consumers, these states should try to expand the outlets for agricultural products from countries that produce them at lowest cost. They should also try to reach agreement on a limitation of export subsidies, one of the field's most conflict-ridden problems.

It is only in the late 1970's that we may reasonably expect fruitful discussions among the United States, Europe, Japan, and other countries on a fundamental overhauling of agricultural production or agreement on common principles of agricultural support. But if these steps occur, they will, at last, establish the preconditions necessary for extending a liberal trade system to the area of agriculture in the 1980's.

Removing Non-Tariff Barriers to International Trade

As tariffs decline in importance, other obstacles to international trade gain weight. A striking number and variety of factors can distort the free exchange of goods and services. GATT has listed 800 such non-tariff barriers.

Every country has developed a considerable number of non-tariff barriers, but these differ, of course, according to national circumstances. In addition to quotas, the non-tariff barriers listed below warrant common study and agreement at the earliest possible date.

There is need for a general review of the multitude of obstacles to international trade which accompany the interventions in complex societies of modern welfare state governments, ranging from taxes to health standards. International action should aim not only at harmonizing these distortions but also at establishing consultative machinery which can help prevent unilateral decisions that will negatively affect international trade. Hence on a number of policy instruments used by modern governments, there is need for prior international consultation before application.

Although the impact of *taxes* on foreign trade has been studied for many years, it is not clear whether arrangements under GATT are sufficient. We do not possess sufficient knowledge about the impact of many taxes. The United States, Western Europe, and Japan should have a major interest in initiating studies in this area within the GATT framework.

Valuation practices have been among the thorniest issues in world trade relations. As suggested above, this problem will disappear if universal reductions of tariffs can be negotiated. But even if such agreement is reached, a transitional period of 10 years lies ahead. This is sufficiently long to require intermediate measures to lessen the impact of certain valuation practices. One of Europe's urgent requests in this connection is early ratification by

Congress of the agreement reached in the Kennedy Round to eliminate the "American Selling Price System."

Government purchase practices are a major factor distorting international trade. In the United States, the "Buy American Act" generally requires that goods be purchased in the United States unless the foreign-made product is between 6% and 12% cheaper. In the field of defense, foreign-produced goods must be 50% less expensive than American products. Some foreign goods may not be purchased, regardless of price. While the American system is relatively open, the Europeans also practice discrimination against foreign goods by administrative discretion, as do some local state authorities in the United States. This entire subject should be reviewed as part of broader American-European-Japanese negotiations so that common practices may be established.

A number of international rules relate to *"anti-dumping duties"* and *"countervailing duties."* Since not all of them are applied in the United States, a common review should be undertaken by Europe, Japan, and the United States in order to assure their universal application.

The field of *standards* of health, safety, and pollution is one of the most complicated and effective obstacles to international trade. Since government intervention in the form of standards is growing constantly, this whole area has become an increasingly impenetrable thicket with a rising impact on international trade. Standards (along with technical regulations and other administrative obstacles) warrant study in the GATT negotiations of 1973 so that present obstacles may be identified and their trade-distorting effect eliminated through common standardization. In addition to coordinating standards, there is urgent need for consultative machinery to be employed *before* standards are adopted as a means of minimizing their effects on international trade.

One final source of distortion in international trade is *subsidies to exports.* These subsidies can take the form of taxes as, for example, in DISC, discriminatory standards, or various economic measures. While some cases are reasonably obvious and could be negotiated, most cases will require thorough common review before agreement can be reached.

A useful approach to these problems would be to examine the *effective protection* resulting from various devices, including non-tariff barriers, tariffs, and quantitative restrictions for specific products, in order to determine priorities for negotiation and possible interim measures to be undertaken prior to tariff eliminations.

Toward an International Approach to Safeguards

The elimination of "voluntary" restraints and non-tariff barriers calls for a new approach to safeguards. The dilemma this poses is not new, but the rise of protectionism in the wake of economic change and interaction makes it more urgent. It would be economically shortsighted to maintain stagnant or backward industries and to distort competition through protectionist measures. On the other hand, prevailing concepts of social justice demand that industries and workers injured by changes resulting from competition be assisted.

Tariffs have traditionally been the main instrument of assistance to stagnant sectors of the economy, but their importance is steadily declining and their place is being assumed by non-tariff barriers, "voluntary" restraints, and various government measures (some of which are barely visible). If Western governments adhere to the basic notion that competition enhances international economic welfare, it is high time for them to focus on the multitude of impediments to competition that have arisen besides tariffs.

States should accept the following basic rules: (1) All hindrances to trade should be reviewed internationally on a continuing basis; (2) they should become subject to international rules which circumscribe their scope and limit their life-span; and (3) they must be accompanied by

internationally-reviewed adjustment programs to aid industries and workers adversely affected by competition, so
that the reasons for initiating the impediments will be
eliminated.

Regulating Multinational Corporations and International Production

We concluded earlier that the spectacular growth of
multinational corporations and international production is
causing a fundamental structural change in the economic
system. As much as 22% of total production in the non-
Communist world is today planned and managed by international companies—with this percentage expected to rise
to 35% by 1980 and 50% by 1990. We would be over-
looking an essential aspect of the international economic
system if we were to focus exclusively on trade and monetary matters, or efforts to improve its functioning.

To be sure monetary reform may diminish some of the
difficulties which appear to stem from capital movements.
The export of American investment capital, a major reason
for the United States balance of payments deficit, is likely
to slow down with a realignment of currencies which
render more expensive the purchase of foreign companies
and assets. Similarly, the outflow of short-term capital—
recently the most important factor in the balance of payments deficit—is likely to be slowed by a more flexible
exchange rate.

With the growing importance of international production,
however, a growing share of international trade will become intra-company trade. This applies today to 30% of
U.S. foreign trade. Since a decision to invest abroad depends on a multitude of factors—many of which cannot
be subsumed under the traditional comparative cost argument, such as political climate, governmental help, growth
potential of the market, etc.—and since foreign investments in turn promote and restructure international trade,
international economic interaction is becoming increas-

ingly removed from the traditional factors that once determined its flow, including liberal trade practices. The operative factors today are internal decision-making by the multinational corporation and the special circumstances under which each operates.

If we assume that multinational corporations and international production are a desirable development because they increase economic welfare, the rising number of these institutions and the significance of their operations require the international community to undertake two tasks:

First, there is urgent need for international agreement on conditions governing international investment decisions. We need rules limiting governmental obstruction and control of multinational corporations. (Japan and, to a lesser degree, France and some under-developed countries have either prohibited specific investments or imposed stringent controls.) On the other hand, since International investment is becoming such a major factor in creating employment, prosperity, and exports, there should be agreement on how far governments can go in attracting or facilitating such investments. This would presuppose a review of various instruments used by governments to support such investments: industrial and regional policies, for example.

There is a second task, no less difficult or important. Though it is argued that certain fears concerning the economic consequences of international investment have been exaggerated,[21] the strength and flexibility of multinational corporations raise many problems for host countries for international interaction. Multinational companies can shift investment capital, determine imports and ex-

---

[21] See Raymond Vernon, "The Economic Consequences of U.S. Foreign Direct Investment," and "Problems and Policies Regarding Multi-National Enterprises," in: *United States International Economic Policy in an Interdependent World.* Papers submitted to the Commission on International Trade and Investment Policy and published in conjunction with the Commission's Report to the President, Washington, D. C.: GPO, July, 1971, Vol. 1, pp. 929-952 and 983-1006.

ports, allocate research funds, sometimes shift profits and taxes, and influence employment to such an extent that they can not only counteract the policies of host governments but create undesirable imbalances.

Democratically elected governments and international organizations are increasingly losing their control over domestic and international economic developments. If this trend is to be halted, the international community must agree on ways and means of regulating multinational corporations which introduce some measure of control but do not stifle this basically desirable new phenomenon.

Much is to be said in favor of a "proposal for the creation by a multilateral treaty of a supra-national authority that would preside over the enforcement of a set of rules regulating the conduct of multinational corporations in host states while, at the same time, prescribing the limits in which host governments might interfere in the operation of such corporations." [22]

Institutions and Procedures: The Need for Policy Coordination

The findings outlined above all point in the same direction: Either we establish effective tools of management and policy coordination to govern the emerging system of economic interdependence, which has brought us unprecedented prosperity and free movement of men, goods, services, and ideas, or the system will be ridden with tensions and ultimately break down.

Much more is at stake than the removal of conventional barriers to economic activity, although such liberalization remains important. Positive action, in the form of internationally-agreed intervention, is required. We must move beyond present multilateral diplomacy and traditional interstate relations in a number of fields; establish new modes of direct contact and cooperation between the

[22] George W. Ball, "Introduction" to Richard Eells, *Global Corporation* (New York: Interbook, 1972), p. 6.

relevant bureaucracies in different countries; accord international organizations a vital role in management; and arrive at a modicum of common planning involving the important countries of the West.

Such change implies abandonment of the sector approach in which particular international organizations or departments deal separately with problems which in reality belong together. Hopefully the preceding analysis has made clear that an effective system for steering today's international economy requires a re-integration of the fields of monetary policy, trade policy, and regulation of international production.

Among the steps required is an overhaul of our institutional framework. There should be regularized contacts between the relevant departments of governments, especially among the European Community, Japan, and the United States, either directly or within international organizations.

OECD should be strengthened to become the center for economic policy coordination. OECD members would, in any case, necessarily be associated with any system of economic decision-making that has the European Community, Japan, and the United States as its centers.

In order to accommodate the necessary reforms, the IMF must be substantially reorganized. But GATT, with minor changes, may be flexible enough to accommodate some of the new tasks advocated above.

In any event, GATT, IMF, and OECD must be brought into a close working relationship in order to achieve the integrated approach which is required today. Reform efforts should review the three bodies in the light of present and future needs, decide upon changes to be effected, on modes of cooperation among them, and on the establishment of new departments (and their locations) within the triangle.

Starting Reform

Time is running out on many of the critical issues in the international economic system. Reform discussions have started on some issues, informally or officially (as within IMF on monetary matters). The next round of GATT negotiations in 1973 will raise a number of problems requiring reform, especially non-tariff barriers.

The United States, the European Community, and Japan should consider two series of measures.

First, they should establish a commission of eminent and knowledgeable private citizens from Europe, Japan, and North America. Its task should be to review the major interdependent problems of the international economic system and develop recommendations for approaches and solutions. The report of the commission should serve to focus public attention and mobilize opinion, invigorate the international dialogue, and provide a working basis for legislatures and governments. Insofar as possible, the commission should be identical in membership with a European-American commission advocated below to review Atlantic future security relations and approaches.

The governments involved should put at the disposal of the commission all necessary expert advice and research facilities as well as making it possible to consult any political or economic group in major countries and international organizations active in related fields. Since it will take some time for the commission to produce its report, a link should be established between its deliberations and the discussions of reform being carried out simultaneously by various international organizations, within countries, and between governments. This will ensure mutual benefits to all concerned parties.

Second, the United States, Canada, the European Community, and Japan should convene a carefully prepared summit conference of heads of state to define, at the highest political level, the basic principles which should in the future govern the international economic system and its management. A summit meeting of this kind would provide the necessary infusion of political determination and will.

Obviously the scope and complexity of the problem, the nature of the required solutions, and the multiplicity of concerned states will make progress on reform of the international economic system extraordinarily difficult. Several years of work will be required. Moreover, the very high price of failure is no guarantee of success. In addition to foresight and patience, the commodity most needed will be political courage, since many of the required solutions will break with the established traditions and patterns of thought. As in the field of security, we must have wide-scale public debate led by courageous political leaders. On both sides of the Atlantic domestic preconditions for the solutions needed are simply very bad. But if these issues are left to a handful of experts, debate will be dominated by the spokesmen for narrow interests. The situation requires a rational presentation of alternatives and a persuasive case for reform in order to create support for new measures among legislators and the public.

2. Strategies of Change

Better Chances for East-West Cooperation in Europe

While relations between post-war allies suffer currently from economic uncertainties and tensions, relations between long-standing adversaries are improving. Not only is the probability of military conflict less than it has ever been since World War II, but the conviction is growing in both East and West that the situation has evolved to a point where relations between the two sides might be put on a qualitatively different level by expanding areas of cooperation and breaking the vicious circle of the arms race.

Especially in Europe, the central focus of East-West antagonism, a mutual recognition of essential interests is creating a moderating effect for the persisting conflicts in interests and goals.

This mutual recognition of essential interests did not come about suddenly, but through a slow and arduous process which began with a change of American policy under President Kennedy. Under the impact of nuclear realities, American policy began to conceptualize what America had already practiced. She refrained from challenging vital Soviet interests through militant confrontation and instead sought areas of common interest which would lend themselves to cooperative arrangements. It was hoped that such cooperation might in the long term moderate the persistent conflict between the superpowers. This reorientation of American policy, subsequently gradually reflected in a similar change in Soviet policy, not only altered the relationship between the superpowers but fundamentally changed the structure of conflict in Europe.

This change was most profound with regard to divided Germany whose problems were potentially the most dangerous. For it was in Germany that the dynamism of unresolved national issues combined with the antagonism between East and West, who faced each other on German soil with high concentration of military power, a situation aggravated by the vulnerability of West Berlin.

The change in the central relationship between the superpowers manifested itself not only in total American restraint during the grave internal crisis in the Socialist camp of 1968 (a repetition of American policy in 1956) but in particular in a variety of bilateral agreements with the Soviet Union, ranging from the Limited Test Ban Treaty to the SALT Agreement and the other arrangements finalized during President Nixon's 1972 visit to Moscow.

As a result of changes in the international environment and in German domestic opinion, Western and West German policy on the German problem began to shift, though slowly. Any Western policy which postulated withdrawal from challenging vital positions taken by the adversary and which instead sought areas of common interest with the East was bound to call into question existing policy on the German problem. This policy was based on three central ideas. First, German reunification should be achieved by dissociating East Germany from the Soviet bloc and integrating it with the Federal Republic along Western democratic lines. Second, the existing Polish border could not be accepted until a peace treaty had been concluded. Third, the process of relaxation of tension in Europe could not begin until the German problem—the most intractable of Europe's problems—was solved.

But Western policy on Germany was not the only challenge to the status quo. It was accompanied by President de Gaulle's unsuccessful attempt to dissociate both Eastern and Western Europe from the superpowers, and more than matched by the Soviet Union's repeated attempts to undermine the status of West Berlin and to interfere in West German politics.[23]

The recent agreements among the Federal Republic of Germany, the Soviet Union, and Poland; the Four Power Agreement on Berlin; and the recent intra-German Basic Treaty signal a significant change of policies in regard to Europe's central problem, Germany. West Germany has today accepted not only the territorial status quo but the existence of two politically different German states, a policy which is being reaffirmed by a variety of intra-German dealings aiming at normalizing relations between the two states. To be sure, improvement of relations across the dividing line remains a central goal of German policy. But it is no longer seen as a precondition to détente in Europe. Rather, it is itself part of the process of détente.

The Soviet Union, in turn, has withdrawn her own challenges to the *status quo*. First, she has withdrawn her claim to a right of intervention in West German politics under the so-called "enemy clauses" of the U.N. Charter— a withdrawal of special importance in light of Western European fears that future danger lies not in open military attack but in Soviet political pressure and intervention.

---

[23] This process of change in Western and West German policy has been examined in greater detail in my *German Foreign Policy in Transition. Bonn Between East and West* (London: Oxford University Press, 1968).

Second, in the Four Power Agreement on Berlin, the Soviet Union, along with a reluctant East Germany, abandoned her policy of separating West Berlin from the Federal Republic. She has explicitly recognized the ties which exist between them and has agreed to orderly procedures for communication and free movement between West Berlin and the outside world.

To be sure, the Berlin Agreement does not eliminate the physical capability of the Soviet Union to challenge West Berlin's ties with the Federal Republic nor does it provide absolute certainty that she will abstain from interfering in West German or West European politics. Nevertheless, the agreement on Berlin, the treaties with the Soviet Union and Poland and the intra-German Basic Treaty have removed some important challenges by each side to the essential interests of the other and have thus defused some of the most explosive issues which in the past have constantly threatened the stability of Europe.

Soviet acceptance of the strong restatement of American and Allied commitment to West Berlin, which the Soviet Union once constantly tested and sought to undermine, is in fact one of the most important (and often overlooked) implications of these agreements. Russia's co-signature on a restatement of America's guarantee and commitment to co-responsibility for peace at one of the most sensitive spots in Europe is a significant step toward Soviet acceptance of an American role in restructuring relations in Europe.

In view of the urgent need for domestic reforms in both East and West, each side is under pressure to reallocate resources from the military to the civilian sector and, hence, to achieve a military balance in Europe at lower cost. The Soviet Union, which has lagged behind the West economically, is increasingly interested in acquiring Western technical know-how as a means of accelerating her own growth. This appears all the more necessary since her economic base is too weak to realize her objective of becoming a power with a global capacity for presence and involvement. Finally, there is every reason to believe that the Soviet Union's concern over Sino-Soviet relations and problems in Asia, demonstrated by the strong build-up of military forces on her Chinese border, is a strong inducement for seeking more stable relations on her western flank.

Both East and West in Europe share a perception of decreased threat from the opponent and a desire to prevent war. The recent East-West agreements in Europe and between the United States and the Soviet Union have further changed attitudes toward the adversary, beliefs about the likelihood of military conflict in Europe, and perceptions of opportunities for positive actions to increase cooperation and stability. A growing number of Europeans are beginning to see some sense and some hope in a long-term view held to date by only a small group of the European Left.[24] Namely, that it may be possible to change the position of the opposite system from threat into challenge, which would mobilize all best resources, and from a deadly conflict into cooperative competition, with each side competing constructively and learning from the other.

While the creation of such a relationship between the Eastern and the Western systems will take many years, there is little doubt that chances have significantly improved for immediate steps toward East-West cooperation. But only concrete negotiations and measures will show whether rising hopes are justified. In addition to MBFR and possibly an enlarged SALT II, a European Conference for Security and Cooperation is now at the center of attention as a possible means of initiating institutionalized East-West cooperation in various fields.

---

[24] For a typical example see: Walter Möller and Fritz Vilmar, *Sozialistische Friedenspolitik für Europa. Kein Frieden ohne Gesellschaftsreform in West und Ost* (Reinbeck bei Hamburg: Rowohlt, 1972), p. 113 ff.

A European Conference on Security and Cooperation: Problems and Prospects

The possibility of a European conference has been mentioned occasionally in East-West pronouncements since the mid-1960's. But it did not become the subject of intensive discussions within the West and between East and West until the NATO Conference of Reykjavik in 1968, at which Mutual Balanced Force Reductions were proposed, and the declaration of Budapest in March, 1969, when a European Security Conference was suggested by the Warsaw Pact countries. The Warsaw Pact countries and NATO have subsequently specified their views on possible subjects for such a conference. Now that negotiations on Germany and Berlin have been successfully concluded, a precondition set by NATO on negotiations for the conference, work was begun in Helsinki in November, 1972 on preparations for the meeting.

Divergent Interests

Both East and West are prepared to use the conference to create a framework in which peaceful change becomes acceptable to both sides. But East and West, as well as the states within each camp, will go to the conference with differing objectives. Whether the interests they have in common will prevail over differences is, of course, not yet known. A striking characteristic of the earlier phase of discussions, before preparations for the conference started, was the dynamic process of shifts in perception and of mutual influencing of attitudes regarding basic issues at the conference. Today, the Soviet Union appears to have renounced her old objective of dissociating the United States from Europe; Western states, in turn, seem less skeptical of the conference as a result of the recent successful East-West negotiations.

The first and most fundamental difference of view between East and West seems to lie in divergent concepts of how peaceful change can be accommodated through new structures of cooperation between East and West. There are also considerable differences of opinion on this point within both camps. Obviously, the Soviet Union would like to see further recognition of the *status quo* and "the results of World War II" and thus consolidate her sphere of influence. It may well be that she conceives such consolidation as a precondition for greater flexibility within her own sphere. The West, of course, is not interested in challenging the *status quo* either, but it will take the present political regimes and security commitments as a point of departure for arriving at new cooperative measures.

The crucial question remains as to how each side defines the limits of peaceful change which will inevitably follow any intensification of economic cooperation and movement of persons, goods, and ideas between East and West. At their Prague meeting, the Warsaw Pact countries proposed that an agreement on renunciation of the use of force should be qualified by the "existing bilateral and multilateral treaties and agreements." This formula seems to suggest that the Soviet Union will want to subject any changes resulting from cooperative agreements to the Brezhnev Doctrine of limited sovereignty among Socialist states.

The problem of defining the framework and limits of peaceful change in East-West relations will arise in connection with virtually every subject raised in discussions of "cooperation," whether it be joint economic ventures, cultural and scientific exchanges, or common environmental programs.

While it would be short-sighted to overlook these fundamental differences in interests, it would also be short-sighted to refuse negotiations because of their existence. The need to open up new channels of East-West communication and cooperation and the desire on the part of some smaller East European countries to enlarge their freedom of maneuver places a moral burden on the West to try to reach agreement with the Socialist countries. The possibility of compromise should not be excluded. Given the rigidity and sterility of past relations between East and West, limited progress would be better than none.

However, change is not a one-way street, nor are its repercussions confined to the side within which change occurs. The Soviet Union may be especially fearful of the consequences for Communist orthodoxy of massive contacts between Eastern European populations and the West, but far-reaching liberalization of movement may pose some problems for the West as well. If accelerated change leads to repercussions in Eastern Europe, there is always a danger of spill over into the West.

What is obvious in the field of security also applies, though to a lesser degree, to possible arrangements in the field of cooperation. While much can be gained from new arrangements between East and West, much can be lost: namely, in international stability. East and West may differ regarding the extent of change desired, but both have an interest in prudent pragmatism.

The second most important divergence of interest between East and West relating to the European Conference arises from possible Soviet intentions to block or slow down West European integration. We shall analyze this problem in a separate chapter. The problem does not solely arise from rigid Soviet hostility to the European Community but from a possible combination of Soviet opposition and weakness within the Community due to disunity among its members.

The third clash of basic interests between East and West often mentioned in connection with the European Conference could result from a Soviet attempt to weaken American links with Europe. It is sometimes said that the Russians seek to induce an American withdrawal which is large enough to leave the Soviet Union dominant in Europe but not so complete as to push the Europeans into a joint conventional and nuclear defense arrangement.

While there is no doubt that the Soviet Union would like to weaken United States influence in Europe, Western fears may nevertheless prove exaggerated if the West insists on maintaining essential links between North America and Europe and if the United States does not itself decide to withdraw from Europe as her traditional sphere of influence. One can detect in Soviet policy a growing appreciation of the stabilizing role of the United States in Europe. This attitude was not only clearly reflected in the Berlin Agreement but appears to have been strengthened as a result of recent bilateral American-Soviet contacts and agreements.

An analysis of potential differences in interest becomes even more speculative if one turns to tactical objectives and procedural questions arising in connection with the conference. Not until the conference enters the working stage can anything be said about the fears and hopes it inspires in East and West. Only then will we see whether some states will seek to turn the meeting into a forum for long speeches and propaganda or whether there is some chance of effective negotiations on concrete issues.

Whether the conference should be a single event, a series of meetings or a permanent process with an institutionalized structure is, of course, more than a procedural question; it is an essential point for the conference agenda.

Issues of the Conference

The conference agenda has been the subject of numerous bilateral diplomatic meetings, communiqués of conferences, unilateral declarations, inter-allied consultations and unofficial studies.[25] East and West now appear to be moving toward agreement on three issues for discussion:

---

[25] For a Western and an East-West collection of articles see: Hans-Peter Schwarz and Helga Haftendorn, eds., *Europäische Sicherheitskonferenz* (Opladen: Leske Verlag, 1970) and "Organisation der Sicherheit und Zusammenarbeit in Europa," papers of a symposium in Vienna, March 10-12, 1972, *Wissenschaft und Frieden,* No. 2, June, 1972 (Vienna: Internationales Institut für den Frieden). For the most comprehensive proposal see: *Some Institutional Suggestions for a System of Security and Cooperation in Europe* (Oslo: International Peace Research Institute, 1972).

first, a common definition of principles governing interstate relations, including renunciation of the use of force; second, political and military aspects of security; third, measures of economic, scientific, and environmental cooperation, as well as cultural exchange. The West is also interested in adding items to the agenda aimed at liberalizing the movement of persons, goods, ideas, and information across the East-West border.

The priority among these issues depends to a great degree on one's conception of the conference and its goals. If the conference is to achieve even limited concrete results at some early stage, the negotiable issues must be dealt with first.

Western states should give priority to those issues on which East-West agreements may be possible. A pragmatic approach which moves in steps from the easier issues to the more difficult also implies a conception of the conference as not merely a single event but as a permanent process which could gradually become institutionalized. The idea that major issues in East-West relations in Europe can be settled in a single conference completely underestimates the difficulties and complexities of the problems that lie ahead.

Principles of Interstate Relations

It is intended that the conference should thoroughly review and formulate principles governing interstate relations, including reciprocity of advantages in mutual dealings, equality, political independence, territorial integrity, non-interference, and self-determination.

This subject could well prove to be one of the most intractable issues to be faced. It can be argued that the need for discussion of these principles, which are contained in the Charter of the United Nations, reflects poorly both on the Charter and on all U.N. members, who subscribe to the Charter and hence to its principles. Nevertheless, a case can be made for introducing principles as an issue for discussion at the conference. Even if the discussion leads only to simple reiteration of principles contained in the U.N. Charter, it will necessarily have involved a thorough review of international politics in Europe and of various grievances and problems in interstate relations. In point of fact, several of the smaller East European states are particularly anxious to submit the theories of limited sovereignty among Socialist states to discussion in an international forum, although their ability and willingness to speak up against the Soviet Union on this issue is widely overestimated in the West.

Moreover, the principles of the U.N. Charter were formulated before the Cold War and without foreknowledge of the special problems which would arise in Europe. It could therefore be meaningful both to discuss the application of these principles to the new situation in Europe and to formulate other principles, not contained in the Charter, which would define long-term goals for common action in East and West that are specific to the European situation. A case could also be made for a Human Rights Convention and a Human Rights Court for all Europe, as now exists for Western Europe.

One of the most interesting unofficial proposals for the conference [26] suggests that it begin with discussion and formulation of principles and then move to their practical implementation through agreements on concrete issues in following years. It is doubtful, however, that such a course would be wise. Any serious discussion of the problem of non-interference or of territorial integrity which goes beyond generalities will undoubtedly run into the difficulty of reconciling Western ideas with Soviet conceptions of limited sovereignty among Socialist states. While an exchange of views on this issue is desirable, it would be a mistake to make agreement on such principles a precondition for further progress of the conference.

---

[26] See *Some Institutional Suggestions for a System of Security and Cooperation in Europe, op. cit.*

The desirable course for Western states would be to introduce the principles of interstate relations at an early stage of the conference as a secondary field of negotiations while giving priority to subjects on which agreements are both needed and feasible.

Political and Military Aspects of Security

The enhancement of security is, of course, a major goal of the conference. But prior to the preparatory meeting in Helsinki, the Soviet Union and the Warsaw Pact states had indicated that they were more interested in those parts of the agenda dealing with cooperation than in the security aspects. They also appear to give priority to a discussion of security in general terms rather than in terms of concrete arms control. Moreover, the Soviet Union did not react for a long time to the Western offer to discuss Mutual Balanced Force Reduction (MBFR).

Despite the Soviet view, it would not be wise to center the European Conference on issues of cooperation while relegating the problems of security to the background. Though it may be true that the East is more interested in the former, the West has a definite interest in the latter. The urgency of the American troop issue, budgetary pressures, and the need to redefine and restate the European-American relationship make it necessary to discuss the question of force reductions from the very beginning of the Conference. The Soviet Union's agreement in diplomatic soundings to consider MBFR separately but parallel to the European Conference improves the prospect for meaningful discussions at the meeting to be held in January, 1973 to which the West has invited the East.

In order to increase the chances of progress on this question, MBFR could be divided into two phases. The first phase should involve a reduction of about 50,000 troops which could be negotiated by concentrating on a relatively quick withdrawal on a simplified process of

reduction. The detailed proposal of MBFR I will be discussed below in the context of analysis of a reorganization
of Western security arrangements. Suffice it to mention
here that Phase I could be dealt with in a group comprised
of the states of the reduction area of MBFR I (Benelux
Countries, CSSR, Federal Republic of Germany, German
Democratic Republic, Hungary, Poland) and the countries
which have troops stationed in this area (France, Britain,
Canada, US, USSR). This group could report from time
to time to the European Conference. In fact, some
involvement of other conference members might be
advisable, if a system of observers to supervise Phase I
reductions can be negotiated and if other conference
members are to participate in the supervisory system.

Independent of MBFR I, the conference should at an
early point focus on the possibility of establishing an
effective system for crisis management in Europe by
agreeing on what constitutes a crisis and by establishing
a flexible institutional framework for dealing with them
through mediation, compromise or other means before
conflicts become too virulent. Such a crisis management
system could be established in the form of a "European
Security Commission," with participation by the United
States, the USSR, and a number of European states. The
commission and its services should be available at the
request of any state in the area or of either of the two
superpowers.

At a later stage in the conference, MBFR II should be
initiated for the purpose of agreeing on rules governing
advance notice of maneuvers and troop movements and
in order to negotiate establishment of a system of observers, constraints on troop reinforcements, the freezing of
defense budgets, of specific arms systems and further
troop reductions. Some of the functions of administration
and supervision could be delegated to the European
Security Commission. Since the issues of MBFR II will
concern a larger number of states and may require their
cooperation on certain aspects, it might be necessary

to enlarge the negotiating committee which has dealt previously with the issues of MBFR I.

East-West Cooperation

The field of new cooperative ventures offers a multitude of possibilities. Always guided by the principle that the negotiable issues should be taken up first, East and West might consider the removal of certain obstacles to increased trade, including tariffs, quotas, and non-tariff barriers. Moreover, they could examine various possible cooperative ventures such as a common energy grid for Europe, the development of new means of transportation, the establishment of a common pipeline system, common industrial ventures, cooperation on a comprehensive environmental program to clean up rivers shared by East and West as well as to save the Baltic Sea.

While both sides could gain much from such cooperative ventures, agreement will neither be easy nor quick because of enormous differences in social and economic systems, traditions, and established thought patterns. Nevertheless, it is imperative to undertake negotiations in this field, not only for the possible gains involved but also in order to erode attitudes of hostility, induce learning processes on both sides, and gradually establish cooperative habits in East-West dealings.

Liberalization of Movement Between East and West

If the advantages of increased East-West cooperation are to be extended to individuals, it will be necessary to liberalize the movement of persons, goods, ideas, and information. The West German government especially is eager to see the normalization of human contacts between the two German states, and a similar development at the European level.

In any event, a modicum of liberalization of movement will be necessary if economic, scientific, and environmental cooperation is to progress. The Soviet government has shown some willingness to move in this direction. Both the Soviet-French Declaration of October 30, 1971, and the Soviet-Danish Communiqué of December 5, 1971, mention an improvement of "contacts between people." Nevertheless, serious differences still exist since there is widespread fear among Soviet leaders that a significant increase in human contacts and in the movement of ideas and information may have undesirable political consequences for them. Only Western patience and perseverance will produce concrete results.

One can envisage a variety of ways in which liberalization of movement could be stimulated, such as the creation of facilities for mass tourism in both directions, student exchanges (accompanied by equivalence of degrees and massive expansion of scholarships for such purposes), all-European TV programs and exchanges of newspapers and books, etc.

Institutional Aspects

Pragmatism and flexibility appear to be the major preconditions for success at the European Conference. The problems involved in establishing the conference as a more permanent process and in creating institutions for implementing agreements must be faced when the time comes. The Conference on Security and Cooperation might establish itself as a regional body of the U.N. General Assembly, with a small permanent secretariat to carry on activities between infrequent plenary sessions.

The main task of implementing agreements should be delegated to permanent sub-committees, particularly the European Security Commission, once the participants have agreed on a system of crisis management, on certain measures of arms control requiring supervision and administration, and on a body that can regularly examine problems of arms control in Europe. This body could be a kind of European Security Council, though without the powers of the U.N. Security Council. Hopefully it would function better than a regional arrangement established under Chapter VIII of the U.N. Charter.

In any event, a link should be established between the European Security Commission and the U.N. system. But it would be premature to define the nature of this link at this stage since this question will require careful study by the members of the conference.

The implementation of various economic agreements could be delegated to the Economic Commission for Europe or, in some cases, to sub-regional organizations such as the European Community or COMECON.

The various arrangements that result from a European Conference should be linked to the U.N. At a time when the international system is undergoing significant change, the United Nations should profit from new measures introducing controls, restraint, and cooperation into adversary relationships. The negligible role which the U.N. has played in stabilizing East-West relations was due not only to the intensity of the East-West conflict—which has since lessened considerably—but also to the reluctance of each side to accord the U.N. a part in resolving the conflict. At the same time, the new measures should not hesitate to question or revise existing U.N. procedures or institutions if this proves necessary. Only in this way can exchange in Europe give new impulses to the U.N. and strengthen it.

The assignment to a newly created U.N. body of certain functions of management, supervision, verification or mediation agreed on by East and West in MBFR might not only facilitate such agreement but also strengthen the U.N. in its peacekeeping function. A European Security Commission, which might verify agreements on force reduction, reinforcement capability, and troop deployment, or act as an observer of troop movements and maneuvers, could be constituted as a U.N. institution. Moreover, if it were located in Berlin it would add a United Nations dimension to the maintenance of the *status quo* there.

Towards a European Security System?

It is often said that the goal of the European Conference on Security and Cooperation should be establishment of a new European security system. Anyone who espouses this goal, unless he takes leave of the realm of practical politics, must opt for the kind of conference which evolves as a long process over many years. Existing antagonisms, with their social, psychological, economic, and military foundations, run very deep. Any attempt to change these structural elements through a political process will require much time and hard work.

Obviously, security should be enhanced during this process. Given the basic characteristics of contemporary international politics, security can be maintained only through effective guarantees with credible sanctions and these, in turn, require the presence of some military means, which should be in adequate balance. In the absence of a U.N. supra-national authority with military force at its disposal—and we are very far from it—guarantees, sanctions and security can unfortunately be assured only by maintaining a core of the traditional instruments of security, namely, commitments within alliances. Hopefully, these will operate at drastically lower military levels and under conditions of reduced threat, with effective machinery for crisis management and arms control.

A new security system in Europe cannot, therefore, dispense with certain elements of the old system for a long time to come, although it will differ from the old system by providing more security. Only after the present antagonism between East and West has disappeared will a completely "new" security system emerge, one that has rid itself of certain aspects of today's structures of alliance, characterized by mutual deterrence. Unless the present state of hostility is replaced by a security community in which the use of force to settle disputes is as reliably excluded as it is today between, for example,

Britain and the Netherlands or France and Western Germany, a collective security system—often cited as the ultimate outcome of present trends—would have no reliable political basis. Establishment of a collective security system should, of course, be the long-term goal and should guide political action in the coming years, *e.g.*, by encouraging East-West cooperation. But the practical answer for the near future lies in an approach which *gradually* transforms the present system.

Western Consultation

When the Federal Republic of Germany entered the active phase of *Ostpolitik* by negotiating a treaty with the Soviet Union, there was considerable fear in the West that Germany's policy would result in a weakening of her relations with the West. These fears turned out to be unfounded, thanks mainly to a far-reaching degree of detailed consultation with the Western Allies at all phases. In fact, there has not been such intensive consultation within the West for many years as there was during negotiations on the Moscow and Warsaw Treaties as well as on the Four Power Agreement on Berlin.

To date there has been a considerable amount of multilateral and bilateral consultation within the West leading to position papers on various issues connected with the conference. Within the European Community, the committee charged with coordination of foreign policy has established a sub-committee on the conference. A second *ad hoc* group, including a commission representative, considers economic aspects of the conference. Within NATO, the conference has been the subject of studies and consultation for over two years.

In the recent past, cooperation within the West and the maintenance of security, and progress in the field of détente have been possible because of effective Western consultation. The Western countries have every reason to maintain intensive consultation at the European and

NATO levels in preparing for, and negotiating at, the conference.

West European Integration and All-European Structures: Opposed or Complementary?

The relationship between progress toward European integration and progress toward European East-West cooperation will be a crucial issue in the coming years. Many West Europeans have not yet faced the dilemmas which these two processes of change raise.

In recent years, integration in Western Europe and the movement toward European cooperation have often been confused. The confusion has been glossed over by such appealing formulas as "the reunification of Europe" or "the European system of economic cooperation."

In looking ahead it is necessary to recognize the essential differences between the movement toward integration in Western Europe and the movement toward cooperation in all of Europe. West European integration—in which, by common agreement economic union is to be followed by later political unity—is a process being carried out by countries with similar political structures and outlooks, on a basis where no single country predominates.

All-European cooperation, however—while aimed at a decrease of tension, arms control, crisis management, normalization of relations, and cooperative ventures—brings together states with antagonistic foreign policy objectives and ideologies and which differ profoundly in the nature of their political regimes, with one state, the Soviet Union, by far outweighing the others in political and military power. The antagonism between Western Europe and the small central European Socialist states may not be so strong as between Western Europe and the Soviet Union, but it is nevertheless a reality.

The conclusion reached earlier about an all-European collective security system applies here as well. Any fully integrated European economic or political system presupposes the disappearance of present hostility and antagonism and profound change, especially within the Soviet Union. The experience of the last two decades shows how difficult it is to effect such change, but the West can encourage this process through a policy of patient cooperation and relaxation of tension with the East.

Although there are significant differences between the processes of West European integration and all-European cooperation, they are not inherently incompatible. They are not alternatives. But if they were presented as alternatives, West Europeans would be extremely short-sighted to sacrifice or slow down the process of unification, trading the prospect of benefits from an all-European system of cooperation for achievements and progress in the field of West European integration. The only sensible way for the Western States to avoid dilemmas which may be raised by the relationship between West European integration and all-European cooperation is to develop policies that make these movements complementary rather than contradictory.

Much will depend on Soviet policy toward the European Community. It has often been asserted that one of the Soviet Union's main objectives in promoting a European Conference is to undermine the European Community. While there is no doubt that the Soviet Union has been and remains opposed to West European integration, on grounds of Communist orthodoxy as well as power politics, there is a chance, if the West remains firm, that she may eventually accept the European Community as a permanent fixture in European politics and even as a possible partner in cooperation.

If one reviews the development of Communist ideology and its theoretical interpretation of West European integration, one sees clearly a trend toward a new interpretation which acknowledges the inherent advantages of European integration and prepares the ground, theoretically, for cooperation with the integrated body. The Italian Communist Party, for example, has advocated cooperation with the European Community without provoking a reprimand from Moscow.

Moreover, one should consider Brezhnev's remarks of March, 1972, in which he said that "the Soviet Union does not ignore the realities of the situation in Western Europe, among them the existence of such an economic grouping of the capitalistic countries as the Common Market." The assertion that the Soviet proposal for a conference was aimed at "undermining the European Economic Community" is an absurd thought. Event if one does not take Brezhnev's remark too literally, another observation made on the same occasion sheds light on what may be the general direction of Soviet policy toward the European Community: "Our relations with the participants of this grouping will naturally depend on their degree of acceptance of the realities which have emerged in the Socialist part of Europe, in particular of the interests of the COMECON members. We are for equality in economic relations and against discrimination." These remarks suggest that the Soviet Union is leaving open the option for a *modus vivendi* with the European Community in the expectation of reaping maximum advantage for herself and COMECON from this prosperous grouping.

For members of the European Community, the answer to the dilemmas raised by the relationship between internal integration and all-European cooperation should be twofold. First, the Soviet Union will desist from any further attempt to challenge this grouping and will finally accept it as a working partner only if the West European nations continue the internal process of integration and move toward genuine economic and ultimate political union.

Firmness in the face of temptations to refrain from further integration, and determination in the face of all possible offensives should, however, be combined with a second policy. The European Community should be flexible enough in its external policy to make it easy for Eastern Europe to negotiate and to initiate practical working arrangements without insisting first on recantations of the political and ideological past. Diplomatic recognition and exchanges of ambassadors are not the main problem. The main task is practical steps toward cooperation. The European Community might even consider moving its Eastern trade departments out of Brussels, perhaps to West Berlin, for a transitional period. Flexibility toward Eastern Europe should also include openmindedness in making liberal trade arrangements with the East European countries, especially the smaller ones which are in more urgent need of trade relations with the Community than is the Soviet Union.

In light of the political and economic achievements of the Community to date and the future potential of West European unification, all-European cooperation can be only a complement to integration, not an alternative. If the Western countries apply this simple wisdom to their policies as they approach the European Conference, both the Community and Eastern Europe can gain from cooperative arrangements. A combination of Soviet pressure on Community members to desist from integration, disunity within the Community, and American passivity *vis à vis* Soviet attempts to weaken the Community would be fatal.

3. Reconciling Change and Security

Peaceful transformation in Europe is the declared goal of all European governments and the superpowers. But, as we have seen earlier, the process of détente, developing arms control measures, and creating new structures of cooperation are not without problems. New forces are unleashed which can render the process unpredictable, and potentially unmanageable, to the point that it may have the opposite effect of what was originally intended.

Policies in the years ahead must transcend Cold War fixations by ceasing to regard the East-West conflict as permanent and immutable and by avoiding the opposite conclusion that security policies involving military means can be abolished as remnants of a reactionary past. Peaceful change must enhance security and, in the short run at least, it must maintain it.

Security in Europe is the result of three interconnected factors: first, the balance of military power; second, the structure of relations among states involved; and third, domestic freedom to pursue the policies of one's choice in conditions adequate for peaceful change without outside interference. A military balance alone is no guarantee or indicator of security. It derives its real meaning from its political context: The political solidarity and identity of interests among allies, the firmness of commitments, and the structure of alliances. Moreover, such factors as the nature of the political relationship between the adversaries and their allies, the degree of tension, and the conflicts or identities of interest provide the setting for security. At the same time, an interpretation which views security exclusively in terms of the probability of military action would be equally misleading, for it would omit the large area of non-military pressures and interference which are of special importance to Europeans.

Between America and Western Europe the institutions and professionals charged with defense pursue their routine efficiently, but debate among the informed public and legislators on the real problems and future challenges to security is either nonexistent, characterized by misperceptions, or ill-informed. What little debate occurs outside of governments characteristically consists of acrimonious and divisive signals among allies, relayed across the Atlantic. It is in striking contrast to American and European preoccupation with China and the Soviet Union, now seen in a generally positive light.

In the United States, despite Administration efforts to the contrary, public discussion appears to presume that the entire security relationship with Europe can be reduced to the simple question of whether or not U.S. troops should remain in Europe, be financed by the Europeans, or be withdrawn. This fixation is mirrored in the West European public, which watches every development across the Atlantic with the nervousness typical of the dependent. Unable to overcome deeply-rooted national myopia, Europeans too have great difficulty in seeing the security problem in a larger perspective.

What Threatens Security in Europe?

Since the outbreak of the Cold War, the probability of aggression in Europe has never been so low as it is today. The fear that the Warsaw Pact countries might contemplate an all-out attack, quite prevalent in the 1950's, has all but disappeared. West Europeans today judge the intentions and attitudes of Soviet leadership as sufficiently rational and pragmatic to consider the probability of aggression aimed at territorial gains or occupation as extremely low. The developments of recent years, particularly the agreements with the Federal Republic of Germany, the Four Powers Agreement, the agreements with the United States, and the initiative for a European Security Conference are seen as evidence of a substantial change in Soviet policy.

It is a moot question whether the change toward a policy of restraint in the Soviet Union can be explained by pragmatism and the peaceful intentions of Soviet leadership or whether the system of conventional and nuclear deterrence built up by the United States and Europe during the post-war period contributed to the prevention of war and the emergence of a more cooperative Soviet policy. Neither case can be scientifically proven, but we take it as a working assumption here that deterrence has played, and still plays, some role in preventing war and in inducing a policy of moderation.

Military capabilities are no reliable indicator of hostile intentions but they do give some indication of the perception of threat and of conceptions of possible military conflict. The ratio of military forces between East and

West remains an essential factor in assessing possible threats to security. Given the immense complexity of any comparison of military capabilities, this assessment should be taken as an approximation, reduced to a few pertinent facts. Using the figures of the International Institute for Strategic Studies (IISS) and of a recent Brookings Institution study,[27] which represent a middle ground between the somewhat optimistic figures of the Pentagon and the pessimistic assessment of military experts in Europe, the situation is as follows.

In 1972 NATO's 5.4 million men in active armed forces (including France and forces stationed all over the world) face about 4.4 million men in the Warsaw Pact forces:[28] But the crucial area is Europe. If one compares NATO forces assigned to Europe, including Britain, France, and Portugal, with the Warsaw Pact forces, including all of the Soviet Union's allies and the USSR troops west of the Ural, NATO's 2,180,000 troops face Eastern troops totalling 2,250,000 men. (Tanks: 12,000 : 41,700.) As the following chart shows,[29] there is a net superiority of 1 : 1.6 in ground forces in favor of the Warsaw Pact between the Baltic Sea and Austria, extending into Western Russia and excluding

MILITARY RATIOS BETWEEN NATO AND WARSAW PACT IN THE CENTRAL REGION OF EUROPE

	M-Day (without France)	M-Day + 30 (with France)
Ground Force	1 : 1.6	1 : 2.1
Tanks	1 : 2.5	1 : 2.9
Tactical Aircraft	1 : 1.8	1 : 2.0

---

[27] International Institute for Strategic Studies (IISS), *Strategic Survey 1971* (London, 1972); IISS, *The Military Balance 1971-1972* (London, 1971), *The Military Balance 1972-1973* (London, 1972); John Newhouse with Melvin Croan, Edward R. Fried and Timothy W. Stanley, *U.S. Troops in Europe, Issues, Costs and Choices* (Washington, D. C.: The Brookings Institution, 1971).

[28] IISS, *The Military Balance 1972-1973, op. cit.,* pp. 4-24.

[29] Taken from Newhouse, *U.S. Troops in Europe, op. cit.,* p. 59.

Bulgaria, Hungary, and Rumania in the East and France in the West. The advantage of the Warsaw Pact increases considerably as more time elapses after mobilization (M-Day), to 1 : 2.1 after 30 days. The shorter geographical distance and the structure of the Warsaw Pact forces make a fast build-up easier than in the West. It is only after a 30-day period, and if no attack occurs to hamper Western reinforcement, that the position of NATO improves in some areas, but overall parity is never reached. The Brookings study estimates that 90 days after mobilization about 2.2 million Warsaw Pact troops would face about 1 million NATO forces.

Although a host of clarifications should qualify this comparison (e.g., the limited reliability of some Warsaw Pact forces in case of war), it shows a clear conventional superiority of the Warsaw Pact in the central region. In the northern area of NATO, the superiority of the Warsaw Pact in ground troops is approximately 5 : 1 if compared with the troops of North West Russia[30] but, because of the uncertain impact of reinforcements by sea or air over long distances by both sides, it is very difficult to assess the exact balance.

The same difficulty exists on the Mediterranean flank of NATO, although for different reasons. IISS estimates show a ground force superiority of NATO of 525,000 : 385,000 men, and a tank inferiority of 2,000 : 5,000. However, the picture changes if instead of counting only six Soviet divisions, as the IISS did, one includes the 28 divisions available in adjacent Russia. Moreover, if one considers that the main Western ground forces are provided by Greece and Turkey, which are themselves at odds and each of which has considerable internal problems, the East-West ratio appears less favorable. If conflict occurs it is most likely to erupt in the eastern part of the Mediterranean thus giving the advantage of short-distance or ground transportation for reinforcements to the Warsaw Pact.

---

[30] Newhouse, *U.S. Troops in Europe, op. cit.,* p. 66.

Finally, the effectiveness of military intervention and the ability to control a crisis differs considerably depending on the position of the respective superpowers, whatever the nominal balance of forces may be since the United States contributes but 10% of the manpower of all NATO forces in Europe, whereas the Soviet Union's share of all Warsaw Pact forces west of the Ural is 66%.[31]

In order to assess the relevance of these military ratios within the wider political context of European security, three types of possible threats to security in Europe will be identified: first, open aggression with conventional forces; second, instability in which military action arises out of smaller incidents; third, outside political interference with the purpose of restricting political choices. We shall consider these potential threats under present conditions and under the assumption that Europe must deal with them alone.

If we consider the first case—open aggression by conventional forces, a contingency which caused considerable anxiety among military planners in the 1950's (e.g., the "Hamburg grab")—the threat to security appears to be extremely low, or non-existent. Three related reasons can be cited. At this stage of East-West relations and Soviet policy, no motive or set of conditions is visible which would lead to such extreme action. Second, any such aggression would be extremely risky for the Soviet Union since it would meet at some—necessarily uncertain—point a tactical nuclear response, with the possibility of escalation to a use of America's strategic nuclear force. Third, such deterrence is made credible by the political and military involvement of the United States in European security, as expressed most significantly by the presence of American troops in Europe; but it is also credible because of the effective Western alliance system, based on a relationship of solidarity and mutual commitment.

---

[31] *Bulletin,* Presse- und Informationsamt der Bundesregierung, No. 97, 30 June, 1972.

For these reasons Western politicians and military planners have accepted Western conventional inferiority as something they can live with. Since the West will never attack, it does not need conventional superiority but only a minimum force to assure defense within the strategy of "flexible response" that can activate nuclear deterrence. Indeed, it could be argued, insofar as overt aggression is involved, that the East-West ratio could even worsen a little without critically affecting Western security, *provided* a credible link to the U.S. nuclear deterrent is preserved.

The second type of threat, which might arise from instability and unrest in East-West relations, creates less predictable situations. In such situations the borderline between military action and political threat cannot be drawn exactly. Possible origins of this type of threat could include, for example, incidents on the access routes to West Berlin, internal disputes among Socialist countries which spill across to the West or a conflict in the Balkans. As we have suggested earlier, détente itself may well trigger a crisis of this kind by unleashing various social and political forces (as was the case, for example, in Czechoslovakia) or by creating extreme disparities in the balance of political and military power between East and West (*e.g.,* as a result of excessive unilateral disarmament).

Such threats and possible responses are unpredictable. But, given the fact that opportunities and goals would be limited and that the initial risks involved for a Warsaw Pact country would be lower, the probability of a threat to West European security arising from these kinds of situations, in light of Warsaw Pact conventional superiority, is greater than the chances of open aggression.

Nevertheless, under present circumstances, three factors keep the risk of this kind of threat within low and acceptable proportions: First, there is the likelihood that any military action resulting from such a crisis would eventually meet the U.S. nuclear deterrence as the crisis escalated. Second, Soviet policy in the recent past, particularly the American-Soviet accords in Moscow, which included agreement on crisis management and the Declaration of Principles, suggest that, at this stage of East-West relations, the Soviet Union is aware of the potential dangers of smaller crises and willing to cooperate with the United States in containing them. Third, under present conditions of American commitment to European security and a well-functioning Western alliance system, conflicts at the periphery affect the entire Western alliance and, for this reason, deter military exploitation of small crises.

A third type of threat, external interference in domestic affairs, takes us farther into the political dimension of security. Such a threat could arise in a situation where Western Europe's economic strength, political cohesion, self-confidence, and relative military strength were so weak that the Soviet Union, exploiting her superiority by a mixture of pressure and threats, might interfere in West European politics, influence political choices and, without ever actually resorting to force, establish a strong and possibly even predominant position in West Europe.

This type of threat has popularly been called "Finlandization," a term which appears inappropriate for two reasons. First, Finland's particular exposure to Soviet pressure is enhanced by both her proximity to the Soviet Union and the fact that she stands alone. Western Europe—further from the Soviet Union and composed of countries with, even in the worst assumptions about the future, some continuing links—is less exposed. Second, the resources and strengths of the West European countries are substantially larger than those of Finland.

Soviet and East German pressure on West Berlin before conclusion of the Berlin Agreement provides a vivid past example of this type of threat. An effort to slow the pace of West European integration could be an example in the future. Perfect equilibrium of military forces is not so important a factor in these kinds of situations as is political strength, confidence, and the certainty of effective deterrence in case détente breaks down.

Although the threat of interference by the Soviet Union remains at the back of Europeans' minds, it is of no real importance at the moment. Western Europe's strength, the momentum of unification, and trans-Atlantic cohesion (as expressed in America's commitments to European defense and her actual presence in Europe) are considerable enough to reduce such a threat to negligible proportions. Only significant changes in the political structure of Western Europe and in its relations with the United States could significantly alter this situation.

This brief assessment of the European security equation has not covered its costs or the doubts it raises for the future. If one includes a quarter of the U.S. defense budget and one-third of the Soviet military budget, the United States, the European members of NATO, and the Warsaw Pact spend approximately $70 billion per year on defense of this area. Given the demand and need for costly social reforms and public investments in both systems these costs are enormous and understandably the subject of growing criticism. Nor should the costs to which one cannot put a dollar sign be underestimated—the psychological burden of fear (although decreasing), the costs of cut-off communications, and the lack of creative competition and cooperation—all typifying a hostile relationship between two systems which could potentially benefit each other (although here again things are changing). Finally, the system is not fool- or accident-proof. War can break out, and its vast potential cost, deliberately elevated as a deterrent to war, would be limitless in reality.

Though it will never be possible to determine exactly whether rational Soviet policy or deterrence has been responsible for preserving relative peace, there is no doubt that the post-war European security system has prevented war. Europeans appreciate all too well this characteristic of the *status quo.* If anyone is to tamper with the present system, he must be very sure indeed that such change constitutes real improvement.

Can Western Europe Maintain its Security Alone?

The general relaxation of tension, reinforced by current balance of payment difficulties, has led to demands in the United States that Europe now handle its security alone. A few European conservatives and men of the Left feebly echo this demand, with the former favoring and the latter strictly opposing the formation of a European nuclear force. Changing American attitudes are well summed up in Senator Mansfield's remark, rebutting former Under Secretary of State Elliott Richardson, "It is all very well to talk about the 'strength, closeness, trust, realism and flexibility' of NATO, as Mr. Richardson did. . . . But it seems to me that there is a contrast between these words and the fact that the 250 million people of Western Europe, with tremendous industrial resources and long military experience, are unable to organize an effective military coalition to defend themselves against 200 million Russians who are contending at the same time with 800 million Chinese, but must continue after 20 years to depend on 200 million Americans for their defense. The *status quo* has been safe and comfortable for our European allies. But . . . it has made the Europeans less interested in their own defense. . . ."[32] Usually demands such as this assume implicitly that Europeans are making an insufficient defense effort compared to that of the United States.

Do Europeans Make a Sufficient Defense Effort Compared with the United States?

Like the earlier comparison of military capabilities between East and West, comparative assessment of defense effort within the West is inherently difficult and can never be exact for lack of universally accepted standards of comparison. In the many years of trans-Atlantic debate on "burden sharing," these problems have been discussed intensely among governments. Nevertheless, a few pre-

---

[32] *Congressional Record*, Daily Ed., April 20, 1970, pp. S 5957-58.

liminary remarks may be in order before taking up the
question of Europe's assuming sole responsibility for its
own security.

In 1970, a year in which the Vietnam War consumed
$16.7 billion of the American defense budget,[33] the United
States spent about 7.8% of its GNP on defense (to be
reduced to 6.4% in 1973),[34] whereas the Europeans spent
about 3.7%.[35] But this gap narrows if we consider three
things. As a result of different political traditions, the U.S.
defense budget contains a number of non-military expenditures, whereas in Europe many military expenditures are
included in the civilian budget. Second, defense simply
costs less in Europe than it does in the United States. In
the Fiscal Year 1972 the United States spent $40 billion
of its defense budget on its personnel of 2.5 million men,
almost twice the entire defense expenditures for general
purpose forces of all European NATO members totalling
2.9 million men. Finally, the United States, unlike Europe,
plays a global role. This results in many additional defense
expenditures unrelated to European security.

In American discussions of defense, it is often assumed
that Europeans can underwrite a relative share of defense
equal to that of the United States. This view not only overlooks the above facts but usually assumes that European
recovery has resulted in a degree of wealth sufficient to
make such a contribution possible. Although Europe has
become wealthy, it is far less wealthy than the United
States. A population of 208 million Americans share a
GNP 50% higher than the GNP of over 300 million NATO
Europeans. If the principle of dividing burdens according
to wealth, which is applied to taxation within Western
societies, were extended to defense expenditure, the dif-

---

[33] Charles L. Schultze *et al.*, *Setting National Priorities, The 1973
Budget* (Washington, D. C.: The Brookings Institution, 1972), p. 73.

[34] *Ibid.*, p. 40.

[35] IISS, *Strategic Survey, 1971, op. cit.*, p. 26.

ference between European and American spending would roughly correspond to the difference in their resources.

Any comparison of American and European defense efforts in Europe depends entirely on what share of the U.S. defense expenditure is assigned to Europe. According to official American sources, total costs of the U.S. commitment to NATO in 1969 (including troops in Europe, U.S.-based forces assigned to NATO and the U.S. Atlantic and Mediterranean Fleets, less the Polaris force), including all costs of annual investments and operations, as well as all indirect support costs in the U.S., amounted to $14 billion. The total cost of the 300 thousand troops stationed in Europe including the Mediterranean, plus their dependents and civilian employees, amounted to about $3 billion.[36]

The European members of NATO spend about $23 billion a year on general purpose forces in Europe, not including British and French Strategic Nuclear Forces and forces assigned to overseas areas. This is one-half *more* than what America's NATO commitment costs, according to official sources.

The West European countries, which have more men under arms in Europe than the United States has for her global commitments, can therefore scarcely be accused of doing less in Europe than the United States, but such assertions increasingly enter into U.S. public debate on these issues.

Behind such views there is often the addtional assumption that the U.S. contribution to NATO in Europe does not really support a common defense system protecting the United States, but a system to defend Europe only. Since this American contribution is allegedly neither recipro-

---

[36] IISS, *Strategic Survey, 1971, op. cit.,* p. 21 ff. A Brookings study rated these costs much higher, *i.e.,* at $25.4 billion for the U.S. NATO commitment and $8.5 for forces in Europe. Charles F. Schultze *et al., Setting National Priorities, The 1972 Budget* (Washington, D. C.: The Brookings Institution, 1971), p. 55. However, the IISS *Strategic Survey, 1971, op. cit.,* p. 22, convincingly argues that this estimate must be too high.

Comparative Defense Resources of an Enlarged EEC, including Norway

	Enlarged EEC	European Alliance members	USA	USSR	Warsaw Pact
Defense Expenditure 1970	$23.1 bill [a]	$24.6 bill [a]	$76.5 bill [a]	$53.9 bill [b]	$61.9 bill [b]
GNP 1970 [c]	$636 bill [d]	$660 bill [d]	$977 bill [d]	$490 bill [b]	$641.5 bill [b]
Def. exp. as % of GNP 1970	3.6%	3.7%	7.8%	11.0%	9.5%
Defense expenditure 1971	$25.25 bill [d]	$23.9 bill [d]	$78.7 [d]	$55.0 bill [b]	——
Defense Manpower (mid-1971)	2,090,000	2,939,000	2,699,000	3,375,000	2,682,000 [j]
NUCLEAR DETERRENCE					
ICBM	—	—	1,054	1,540	
IRBM/MRBM	9	9	—	700	
SLBM/SLCM	80	80	656	830	
Strategic bombers	36	36	360	140	
MAIN COMBAT VESSELS					
Submarines					
Missile, nuclear [e]	5	5	41	70	
Missile, diesel [e]	—	—	—	56	
Attack, nuclear	7	7	53	25	
Attack, diesel	91	109	46	210	
Attack carriers	4	4	15	—	
Other carriers [f]	5	5	3	2	

Missile cruisers/destroyers	33	33	73	50	
Other escorts [g]	148	181	148	176	
MAIN BATTLE TANKS [h]	5,343	6,650	1,100	11,600	23.350 [k]
TACTICAL AIRCRAFT [i]	2,800	3,600	8,500	8,700	10,336 [k]

Notes:
[a] NATO definition except Eire.
[b] See *The Military Balance 1970-71* pp. 10-12 for calculation of these figures.
[c] OECD estimates.
[d] At 1970 official exchange rates.
[e] Ballistic and Cruise Missiles.
[f] ASW, Commando, and Helicopter Carriers.
[g] Cruisers, destroyers, frigates, and other non-coastal escorts.
[h] In the European theatre only.
[i] Combat aircraft of all Services.
[j] Includes 50% of all Soviet forces.
[k] Includes Soviet forces in the European theatre.

cated by European support for the United States in other
areas, particularly the trade and monetary fields, nor
needed, in view of relaxed tensions, some conclude that
it can be dispensed with.

But this line of argument misses the crucial point by
viewing European security in narrow terms of defense and
of troop and weapons ratios, instead of seeing security for
what it is today more than ever, a political and military
structure that maintains stability and allows for peaceful
change without unwanted outside interference. Europe's
future security problem does not lie primarily in the conventional military balance but in the political context which
stabilizes the military balance and makes mutual force
reductions possible.

Can Europe Maintain Its Security Alone?

A first glance at the defense capacity of Western Europe
suggests that Europe has a reasonable chance of defending itself alone. Its resources are considerable, even by
superpower standards. If one adds up economic and
military capabilities in a number of fields (see the table
below), Western Europe measures up quite respectably
to Eastern Europe.[37]

In order to discuss security in all its dimensions and
Western Europe's capability to go it alone, we shall posit
as a hypothetical case a course which is quite frequently
advocated in the U.S. and more or less openly feared by
a number of Europeans. We shall assume that the United
States withdraws all its troops from Europe and the Mediterranean but that she leaves the military materiel required
to arm reinforcements in time of need and that she maintains a nuclear guarantee for Western Europe with her
strategic nuclear force.

Such withdrawal of American troops would increase the
superiority of the Warsaw Pact countries within the Central

---

[37] Taken from IISS, *The Military Balance 1971-1972, op. cit.,* p. 8-11;
IISS, *Strategic Survey, 1971, op. cit.,* p. 26.

and Northern areas of Europe from 1 : 1.6 to 1 : 2.4. More-over, the forces withdrawn would be among the best equipped and best trained in Europe.

The change in the conventional ratio would not in itself be crucial. What matters is something else. The sub-stantial increase in conventional superiority of the Warsaw Pact countries would render even more important those factors which have hitherto been meant to counterbalance such superiority; America's political and security com-mitment to Europe, as expressed through the U.S. pres-ence and its direct link to the U.S. Strategic Nuclear Force. Complete removal of all troops would drastically under-mine the credibility of the U.S. nuclear guarantee. Such a withdrawal would, therefore, have an effect on security in Western Europe which far exceeds a mere change in troop ratio in favor of the Warsaw Pact states.

If we turn to the first type of possible threat identified above, all-out aggression, an assessment must depend on the assumptions one makes about Soviet policy. If one applies the prevalent notions of strategic thinking, Ameri-can withdrawal from Europe would change the military balance in favor of the attacker. The conventional superi-ority of the Soviet Union would be complemented by nu-clear superiority in tactical and strategic weapons which could encourage a preemptive strike on the nuclear forces of Britain and France, followed by a conventional attack. British and French nuclear forces are not an effective substitute for the American nuclear deterrent, which is activated by involvement of U.S. troops on the front line. Not only would these two nuclear forces be infinitely less effective in size and technology, as well as far more vulner-able, but their credibility and, hence, their deterrent effect would be lower since French and British troop involve-ment outside their own borders does not equal that of the United States which has spread half a million of its na-tionals—soldiers, dependents, and civilian employees—around the critical areas of NATO.

There is reason, however, to question such conventional strategic wisdom. Even if the Soviet Union could eliminate the British and French nuclear deterrents through pre-emptive strikes in order to mount a conventional attack, the present state of East-West relations and current Soviet policy relegate such a contingency to the realm of the barely possible. Reckless adventurism of this kind is not conceivable under present circumstances. Even if, tech-nically, the U.S. nuclear guarantee were not totally cred-ible, it would at least remain uncertain. Only a victory for irrationality in Moscow and total estrangement between the United States and Europe could lead to a situation where the Soviet Union might be temped to use the *threat* of such aggression as a means of extracting concessions from Western Europe. But such a future is extremely im-probable. We can conclude then that in terms of all-out aggression, an American withdrawal of conventional troops would have relatively limited impact *provided the nuclear guarantee and a working relationship between Europe and America are maintained and Soviet policy continues to develop along present lines.* If the latter factors change, however, withdrawal would unsettle the situation.

Withdrawal of American troops would have its greatest effect on the maintenance of security in a framework of crises of instability and external interference. In the case of crises of instability, military action would be limited, if not absent, at the beginning. If the United States were no longer present, the Soviet Union would not be required to take the same precautions for avoiding direct confronta-tion with the United States—undoubtedly a major consider-ation for the Soviets—since she would not encounter the physical presence of American troops. Moreover, Soviet moves and goals might be too ambiguous or limited for the United States to risk activating the nuclear guarantee for Europe in a credible manner.

It is doubtful that the possibility of reinforcing the Euro-pean NATO members by U.S.-based troops in times of crisis would sufficiently improve the situation. As has been suggested in the intensive debates among experts, the dispatch of troops across the Atlantic would sharply increase the degree of tension in a crisis. Consequently it becomes an instrument of rather dubious value. To bring American troops over only in time of need is of little use in crises where the adversary's objectives remain unclear or in a sudden crisis with quick, limited military action.

Various past crises in the Middle East and Berlin suggest that a withdrawal of American troops would undermine European security in what is the most probable type of conflict, namely, crises of instability. How could Western Europe withstand an attack on, or a gradual strangulation of, Berlin—whose loss would have a profoundly disruptive effect on Western Europe—without America's political guarantee (reiterated in the recent Berlin Agreement) backed up by U.S. involvement and U.S. presence?

The effects of total American withdrawal on possible threats to European security by external interference would be even greater than in a crisis of instability. An important assumption is involved here. It is hardly conceivable that a withdrawal of American troops could occur without causing in its wake considerable strains and without undermining Europe's confidence and stability. To be sure, this would not be sudden but probably would evolve gradually, with European states reacting in various ways, ranging from calls for unity, rearmament, and isolated accommodation with the Soviet Union. In any event, the political environment in Europe would be profoundly disturbed by such a withdrawal. It would leave open the possibility of gradual interference by a Soviet Union which no longer confronted a self-confident Europe, united in its defense policies with the United States.

One may rightly deplore a spirit of dependence on the part of Europeans which causes them to underrate their own strength and to insufficiently develop and pool their own resources. But the dependence is a fact, whether one likes it or not, and so is the resulting mentality. The substantial erosion of confidence and strength caused by

withdrawal of American support is likely to have an increasingly disruptive and snow-balling effect if a limited
military crisis were to break out or Soviet pressure be
exerted.

What we have said about different types of threats to the
Northern and Central region of Europe also applies to the
Mediterranean, although the situation there is even more
complex than in the North. Numerically, an American withdrawal would only reduce Western superiority. For the
time being, the Soviet Fleet in the Mediterranean is still
smaller than the fleet of Italy alone. But the level of
Western superiority is less certain on closer inspection.
Moreover, in view of possible repercussions from the Arab-
Israeli conflict and the uncertain future of some Balkan
states, conflict is more likely to erupt in the Mediterranean
than in Central and Northern Europe. In addition, as the
functioning of the industrial societies in Western Europe
and the United States increasingly depends on oil imports
from this area, the Mediterranean is bound to assume
growing importance. For this reason the impact of
an American withdrawal becomes at once more unpredictable and more momentous.

Given Western Europe's considerable resources, is there
no possibility of her assuming sole responsibility for her
own security? She would probably be able to do this if
two conditions are fulfilled. First, there would have to be
a genuine union of Western European states involving a
common economic, foreign, and defense policy, based on
solidarity and sufficient strength to act according to common goals. Second, Europe would need a nuclear force
subject to a genuinely common defense policy and the
decision-making of a united European government. This
force could be much smaller than the nuclear forces of the
Soviet Union and the United States but capable of surviving
a first strike and to do enough damage to deter Soviet
military intervention in West Europe.

Both conditions are unfulfilled. Unification is still in its
early stages and, deplorable as it is to Europeans, the

ingrained traditions of different nations make the process of unification very slow. Without unification and a common foreign and defense policy, the numerical strength of European armed forces only amounts to the sum of separate national forces. It is by no means as effective as it would be if it were the integrated instrument of a united Western Europe. The absence of adequate European cohesion, therefore, has a particularly crucial effect on the problem of future external interference and instability in Europe.

Any attempt to accelerate European unification by simply handing over to the Europeans responsibility for their own defense, confident that their will to survive will make them overcome their differences in a unanimous act of solidarity, is likely to be counter-productive. The transfer of certain security functions to Western Europe and a stronger and more deliberate European effort in this field could undoubtedly become elements of a new approach for the future, provided that they are undertaken jointly and after careful consideration. But a policy of transferring responsibilities to a group which cannot assume them simply diminishes the security of everyone.

The second condition for an autonomous European defense, the establishment of a European nuclear force, is not fulfilled either. Unlike the goal of European unity, it is not even considered desirable by most Europeans. Apart from the fact that without American technological help— which is by no means guaranteed—the creation of a European nuclear force would take many years, its formation would probably raise more problems than it solves. Complete political unification and solidarity would be required before this most difficult of all political decisions could be delegated to a common institution. Since the military field is likely to be the last to be integrated in the process of unification, it will take a long time to create this precondition. More important, it will be impossible for many years to come to square the circle of West Germany's nuclear participation, which now neither the Germans nor the other Europeans want, while, at the same time, avoiding discriminating against Germany. Finally, since the formation of such a force is likely to meet vigorous Soviet resistance and sharpen East-West tensions, its creation would undermine rather than increase European security.

It is therefore doubtful that America would be wise to encourage a European nuclear force. As an American observer put it: "For the United States actually to support the nuclear development of Western Europe and Japan, in the hope of being ultimately relieved of its role as nuclear guarantor, and in the conviction that the present central balance makes any Soviet or Chinese retaliation impossible would sacrifice, if not nuclear peace, at least the chances of moderation and détente to a distant and dubious pentagonal nuclear 'balance'." [38]

Since the preconditions for an autonomous European defense are unfulfilled in the case of European unity and undesirable in the case of a European nuclear force, European security cannot be maintained without active American involvement and presence. Even if many Americans, like most Europeans, conclude from the continuing détente that Soviet intentions have become less hostile, it would be premature to assume that military conflicts will no longer occur. Even if the probability has decreased to a 1% chance, we need an insurance policy for that 1%. Otherwise, as the experience of the 1930's in Europe showed, the 1% probability may rise to a more dangerous level. Defending American military involvement in Europe or European troop levels on the basis of the probability of all-out aggression or in terms of troop ratios, as some still do, begs the real issue of European security.

The most significant European security problems in future are likely to arise from crises of instability and from attempts at external interference. Although the nature of these threats will make possible a number of adjustments, including some military reductions, a major American and

---

[38] Stanley Hoffmann, "Weighing the Balance of Power," *Foreign Affairs* (July, 1972), Vol. 50, No. 4, p. 622.

European security effort will nevertheless still be required. Recent years have offered no grounds for belief that traditional power politics have suffciently disappeared within the Soviet Union to make a common Western security effort unnecessary.

American and European Interests in Europe's Security

If we begin by examining *American interests* in European security, it must be said at the outset that a definition of such interests is, of course, up to the Americans themselves. Because America is today reassessing her role in the world, it is difficult to discern a clear consensus, let alone future results of the present debate.

But we can take as a working hypothesis that the two basic interests which have guided American foreign policy in the past will continue to shape her future role in the world. The United States will not permit any area vital to the international constellation of power to fall under the influence of her main competitor, the Soviet Union. Second, the preservation of stability in such areas is vital to her own interests. Even if America further reduces her involvement in the world, Europe will probably remain a region essential to American interests because of its strategic position and resources.

Since Western Europe alone will not be able to maintain security and stability in this area essential to the United States, it is in America's interest—even with reduced world involvement—to participate actively in the organization of European security, backing up her political commitment by maintaining some physical military presence and, in the economic field, the kind of cooperative relationship which she herself needs for her own prosperity in an interdependent international economy.

To date the American presence in Europe has been a major factor in preventing war. The burden of proof that security can be maintained without that presence should be borne by those who advocate its reduction or withdrawal.

If these conclusions are correct, the current debate between America and Europe is being dominated by two false issues.

First, total U.S. withdrawal, given this reading of American interests, should not even be an issue. Those Americans who understandably and justifiably advocate reduction of America's overseas involvement in light of the Vietnam tragedy must ask themselves whether the redefinition of America's role in the world should be carried to the extreme of withdrawal from Europe, and whether they are willing to face the prospect of instability in that critically important area of the world.

In internal American debates, advocates of U.S. withdrawal from Europe often fail to see that withdrawal will probably *not* result in any significant reduction of American defense expenditures. Rather, it might lead to increases. A gradual reduction of the size of American forces in response to reduced threat, decided upon in careful consultation with her European allies and implemented in an orderly fashion, is one thing, but a unilateral withdrawal which leaves behind an unstable Europe is quite another. It is highly doubtful that America could in fact dissolve all the divisions she had assigned to Europe even if they were shifted to the United States. Withdrawal under such circumstances not only would represent no gain to American security but would undermine the cooperative basis of the European-American relationship, necessary for reordering the international economy in coming years.

Withdrawal would also raise serious questions in regard to America's commitments as one of the Four Powers in Berlin and in relation to the German problem. Since Germany is located at the center of Europe, where East and West meet with the highest concentration of military power, and since West Berlin remains particularly vulnerable, this area will continue to be crucial to world peace. To argue—as some Americans and Europeans do—that these commitments, derived from World War II and the Cold War, are now obsolete and should be shelved as the remnants of a dark past is simply to overlook the continuing existence of many insecurities and threats, even though the Cold War, in its previous form, has disappeared.

As long as the East-West conflict persists, Central Europe will continue to require prudent attention and careful security measures. The new Berlin Agreement among the Four Powers was negotiated by the United States mainly with a view to the future as a means of improving conditions for stability and peace in Europe. But the new commitments to West Berlin and stability in Central Europe cannot be fulfilled in times of crisis unless they are supported by a sizable presence.

Most important, the idea of complete withdrawal overlooks the fact that maintaining the *status quo* in Europe would be in America's national interest even if relations with Western Europe became less friendly. The United States would suffer a severe set-back if the resources of Europe slipped into the Soviet sphere of influence. That applies also to the southern flank and the Mediterranean. The Sixth Fleet participates in securing not only European but America's national interests. This force is a major element of American influence in the Mediterranean, particularly insofar as the Arab-Israeli conflict is concerned. It also plays a major role in U.S. competition with the Soviet Union. To a growing degree, the Sixth Fleet will secure shipment of Middle East oil supplies on which the United States will become increasingly dependent. Even without NATO commitments, these U.S. forces would almost certainly be in that area. For these reasons, advocates of withdrawal from Europe ignore the fact that the security of Europe is in the common interest of America and Western Europe.

If this interpretation of American interests is correct, discussion of financial savings resulting from complete withdrawal is based on false issues. Since a complete withdrawal of all 300,000 troops from the Mediterranean and Western Europe would decrease stability in those areas, little or no money would be saved, because it would almost certainly be necessary to maintain these units fully or partially in the United States owing to the worsened European situation.

Moreover, the effect of American troop presence in Europe on the American balance of payments has been exaggerated. In 1971 Senator Symington observed, during the debate on the Mansfield Amendment providing for withdrawal of American troops: "U.S. defense expenditures in Western Europe which entered the international balance of payments in the fiscal year 1970 totalled $1.731 billion, the highest figure ever for such expenditures. In order to place this figure in perspective, let us note that our balance-of-payments deficit in 1970 on a liquidity basis was $3.85 billion; therefore, our military expenditures in Western Europe accounted for 46.1 percent of all that deficit. If military sales to Western Europe, which I am informed totalled $599 million in 1970, are deducted from the $1.77 billion of military expenditures in Western Europe, net military expenditures still constitute 30.5 percent of the total balance-of-payments deficit in 1970."[39]

Apart from the fact that the balance-of-payments deficit rose from $3.85 billion to $29.8 billion in 1971, this view misreads the order of magnitude of the various factors influencing the U.S. balance of payments. Many are more decisive than military expenditures. In 1970, American exports amounted to $42 billion while imports totalled $40 billion. Income from U.S. investment abroad added up to $8 billion ($9.3 in 1971), and the net outflow of private capital was $6 billion.

It is difficult to understand why the United States has spent up to $20 billion a year and thousands of American lives on the defense of Vietnam—an area which a growing consensus regards as not essential to American interests—while objecting to annual expenditures of $3 billion in support of a vital area. Nevertheless, Europeans must recognize that the maintenance of an American presence

[39] *Congressional Record,* Daily Ed., May 19, p. S7395.

in Europe constitutes a genuine problem insofar as the U.S. balance of payments is concerned. But a solution of this problem should be reached primarily through international economic reform which will hopefully terminate America's chronic balance of payments deficits of recent years. An agreement on burden-sharing in a new multinational form to offset America's military expenses in Europe would then play only a secondary role.

If we turn now to *European interests,* it is obvious that the maintenance of a viable security link with the United States remains essential, although there is need for the establishment of a different organization and better conditions for maintaining this link. In this connection three aspects of European interest are particularly relevant.

First, any reorganization of U.S.-European security should more adequately reflect the increased weight, identity, and growing unity of Western Europe and should provide for a European contribution to an alliance which supplants the former concept of an Atlantic community in which a single United States was associated with a number of smaller European allies and one Canadian ally. The new concept of alliance should involve a bilateral partnership between Europe on the one hand, the United States and Canada on the other.

Second, it is essential that Europe create preconditions which will enable France to participate fully in any European defense contribution to an Atlantic partnership.

Finally, it is in Europe's interest that whenever American-Soviet negotiations relate to European security or European-American relations, they be thrown open to others concerned with the problems being discussed.

America's and Europe's common interests in a reassessment of their security relations have three aspects. Both Europe and America want cheaper security by decreasing their defense budgets if this can be done without upsetting stability, and by reducing risk through détente, cooperative ventures with Eastern Europe, and arms control. Secondly, it is in the interest of both to close the endless debate on troop stationing and withdrawals and discontinue the accusations which have been erosive and divisive. They should instead examine the present situation together in order to find an adequate and relatively permanent solution for the security dilemma of both sides.

Third, the United States and Europe have a mutual interest in pursuing simultaneous solutions in the security and economic fields. Not only has each field had a somewhat neglected but highly negative impact on the other but a solution to one requires a solution to the other.

Finally, America and Europe should stop looking at their security efforts in the traditional terms of an East-West confrontation. Instead, they should undertake a common effort to build a lasting international structure in Europe which will maintain peace while allowing for change.

Elements of a New Approach

The preceding has shown that the time has come for a fresh look at the European-American security relationship, as well as the goals which should govern such a reassessment. In examining a new approach, let us now consider, consecutively, possible machinery for initiating and sustaining a reassessment of new measures, the prerequisites for, and participants in, any discussion of the issues involved, and, finally, the specific measures to be considered.

Machinery of Reassessment

If governments on both sides of the Atlantic agree with the conclusions outlined above, they will obviously require political machinery to deal with the issues raised by security in coming years and to examine future steps. Some of the steps worth considering are identified below. Needless to say, other measures are conceivable.

It would be highly useful to create an informal and effective European-American commission of eminent and knowledgeable private citizens to examine the factors governing security in the Atlantic area and to recommend security policies for the future. The commission should focus attention and mobilize opinion, invigorate the trans-Atlantic dialogue, and provide a working basis for action by legislatures and governments.

In order to make sure that security is seen in relation to the problems of international economic reform and policy coordination within the Atlantic area, this commission should be, insofar as possible, identical with the commission advocated above to review current problems in international economic reform and to recommend solutions for the future.

Participating governments should put all possible expert advice and information at the disposition of this commission. It should work outside established institutions, such as NATO, in order to make a fresh beginning and to facilitate French participation. It should be free to establish subsidiary bodies to deal with specific issues and to tap the expertise of existing institutions.

In view of the importance of discussion among members of the informed public on both sides of the Atlantic, the commission should consider at an early point in its work when and in what form representatives of legislatures should become involved so that favorable conditions will be created for democratic consensus on all measures to be recommended.

At an appropriate time, an Atlantic summit conference of heads of governments should be convened in order to define the outlines of future security policy in the Atlantic area and to provide political impetus for new steps.

Debate and Consensus

There is great need in both America and Europe for political leaders to stimulate debate on these issues. While it may be easier to settle many problems through high-level private talks and quiet diplomacy, it is crucial to complement such actions by public discussion aimed at remedying the present state of public ignorance by presentations of the facts and of possible choices for the future.

Americans and Europeans will have to face some un-comfortable facts in this regard. In the United States, the relationship of trust which once existed between foreign policy leaders, on the one hand, and Congress and public opinion, on the other, has been disturbed considerably by the Vietnam War and other factors. As a result there is greater need for public support of any new policies so that these may be assured of the degree of certainty and con-tinuity that is required for the future.

Moreover, the few voices raised in public debate out-side of government in America too often represent specific interests which are unable or unwilling to take a long-term view or to see their interests in a wider perspective. There is little careful analysis of the middle ground between the extremes of defending the *status quo,* and of radical change through total American withdrawal from outside commitments.

A similar situation can be found in Europe. There is insufficient informed discussion between those—particu-larly the young—who think the time has come for dumping all military security and those who, partly in reaction, cling all the more rigidly to the *status quo.* There is far too little attention to the middle ground and to a gradual approach to present problems.

There is no point in hammering out solutions among governments and a small élite which would not then be supported by legislatures and the public. The democratic traditions of both America and Europe require that reorga-nization of their mutual relationship and of their respective roles in the world be endorsed by democratic consensus among their legislatures and the public. Moreover, in the security field, continuity, and a modicum of certainty are indispensable. Not only would the Europeans like to see an end to uncertainty about America's commitment to their mutual security, but the Americans, in turn, want a clearer and more certain understanding of Europe's contribution. The establishment of such an atmosphere of reasonable predictability and trust in the future will be indispensable in order to resolve the difficult economic and financial problems which Europe and America share.

MBFR I: A Troop Reduction of 50,000 in the Central European Region

A first and relatively speedy phase of Mutual Balanced Force Reductions between East and West could seek a decrease of about 50,000 troops on each side in the Benelux Countries, West and East Germany, the CSSR, Hungary, and Poland. Of that amount 80% could be allotted to a withdrawal and dissolution of American and Soviet troops and 20% to a dissolution of other NATO and Warsaw Pact troops located in these countries.

Such a procedure solves a dilemma. On the one hand it would satisfy strong pressures on the U.S. Administration to reduce the volume of American troops in Europe and would do so in an orderly and mutually agreed on fashion, on the basis of reciprocity by the Warsaw Pact countries. On the other hand, it would accommodate a desire held by both NATO and the Warsaw Pact to lower the cost of security without upsetting the balance of forces or becoming bogged down in the various aspects of MBFR which are so complex and difficult that they will take years to resolve through East-West negotiations.

MBFR [40] has been under intensive discussion in the West ever since NATO proposed negotiations on balanced troop reductions to the Warsaw Pact countries at their 1968 Council meeting. While there are differences of opinion among NATO members on various aspects of MBFR, it can be said that three goals may be common to the West as a whole. First, MBFR could help to limit the Soviet Union's capacity for intervention and control in Eastern Europe. Second, MBFR could help reduce military con-

---

[40] We follow here in part the comprehensive analysis by Christoph Bertram, "Mutual Force Reductions in Europe: The Political Aspects," *Adelphi Papers,* No. 84 (London: The International Institute for Strategic Studies, 1972).

frontation and create a balance at a lower level of military strength. Finally, MBFR could be a complementary area of negotiation, as well as a testing ground, in the political process of détente between East and West.

There are five different problems connected to MBFR, of which reduction of troop level is only one:

1. Agreement on principles to serve as the basis for security in Europe, in the form of a "code of conduct" among states; *e.g.,* principles of non-intervention, non-use of force, etc.;

2. Constraints on military deployment (such as general military movements, maneuvers, reinforcements in time of crisis, etc.);

3. A force limitation agreement (a freeze on specific types of military forces);

4. The reduction of forces; and

5. Establishment of a system of verification.

Each of these subjects poses very different and highly complex problems. For example, how can balanced reduction be achieved when the Warsaw Pact countries have a natural geographic advantage because of the shorter distances required to obtain reinforcements? How can the thorny problem of verification be solved, given traditional Soviet opposition to any on-sight inspection? How can different weapons systems and different types of forces be compared? Behind each of these questions are delicate political problems, such as the influence of the respective superpowers, the internal cohesion of the respective alliances, the kinds of military strategy to be employed, etc.

If the West pursues too adamantly through MBFR the objective of inducing political change within Eastern Europe, its progress could be very slow, for such intentions would meet with deep Soviet distrust. Moreover, agreements to limit military deployment and restrict the capability to intervene would also pose serious problems for the Western states since they are more dependent on reinforcements in time of crisis than are the Warsaw Pact countries.

The proposition that MBFR can be a major instrument for inducing political change must be seriously questioned. In most of its aspects, such as the non-use of force or genuine restraints on military movements, progress will be possible only when political conditions are ripe. Realistically, MBFR can be little more than a series of measures which reflect and accelerate the political process of improving East-West relations.

The preceding proposal is based on the assumption that MBFR can take place in two phases. In the first phase, one particular aspect—the reduction of troops in the countries of central Europe—would be the subject of negotiation and agreement. If the more complex problems of geographical asymmetry, verification, general principles, constraints, etc., are removed from the center of negotiations—although they cannot be entirely neglected—negotiations should have a reasonable chance of success within a limited time. In order to facilitate negotiations and to avoid any detrimental precedent, it should be made explicit that any solution agreed on in the first phase should not prejudice any step or approach to be taken in the second.

During the second phase of MBFR, when, hopefully, the political situation in Europe will have improved as a result of the first agreement, the more complex and political aspects of MBFR can be negotiated. A considerable amount of time will undoubtedly be required before such negotiations produce results.

While the number and location of troops to be withdrawn will have to be determined through study within the West and negotiations with the East, the general order of magnitude we recommend implies a substantial reduction of American troops. If each side reduces by 50,000, the resulting withdrawal of 40,000 American troops would amount to a 13% reduction of all American troops stationed in Europe and the Mediterranean and to an 18%

reduction of troops stationed in the central and northern region of NATO. The reduction suggested here would be implemented in the central and northern areas and would decrease the number of American troops, mainly those stationed in Germany, to about 180,000.

Although the proposed reduction of 50,000 would further increase the conventional superiority of the Warsaw Pact countries in central Europe, the increment is small enough not substantially to undermine Western security in respect to the different types of future threats possible within Europe. The effectiveness of America's commitment would not appear to be substantially weakened, although it might approach its lowest tolerable threshold. The effectiveness and credibility of this commitment would be more assured if simultaneously a long-term concept of the European-American security relationship can be agreed on in the near future.

Selection of the Benelux Countries and the Federal Republic of Germany in the West, and East Germany, the CSSR, Hungary, and Poland in the East would confine the reduction to an area where the high concentration of ground troops makes reduction somewhat less intractable than in the northern and southern flanks, with their higher importance of naval and air forces. Although the eastern area would be larger than that of NATO, selection of these countries would simplify matters considerably by avoiding the complex issue of achieving balance through symmetry in reductions. At this stage NATO can tolerate an identical numerical reduction by East and West in the proposed area. But at a later stage and at lower military levels, the question of balance must be approached in a more thorough fashion by creating packages of various measures to achieve an equilibrium that is acceptable to both sides.

The preceding proposal of a first-phase reduction of troops includes about 20% European troops (10,000). Their participation appears necessary not only in order to give them a share in the savings involved but also in order to insure adequate European participation from the very first step of MBFR. If the need arises, savings resulting from troop reductions can be used by Europeans to finance European contributions to European-American undertakings covered in a general financial agreement.

The European-American Commission mentioned earlier could help prepare for the first phase of MBFR by making use of work done so far within NATO. But the negotiations themselves to be effective must be conducted by the governments of countries with troops in the reduction area. This implies participation not only of countries in the reduction area and the superpowers but Britain, Canada, and France. Participation by Britain and France appears important both as a means of accommodating French concerns that MBFR might erode Four Power responsibility for Germany and because they are the two major military powers in Western Europe outside the countries of the reduction area.

A Reassessment and Restatement of the European-American Security Relationship

An examination of the security situation in Europe and the nature of American security commitments resulting from it seems imperative. Given the relaxation of international tension and the neo-isolationist criticism of American security policy in Europe—partly a spill-over from criticism of involvements elsewhere—only a rational assessment of the situation, combined with the presentation of a security policy that is persuasive to Congress and the American public, can put an end to that criticism and provide the consensus necessary for certainty and policy continuity.

President Nixon's Administration has been trying to build the consensus for a foreign policy which implies a changed and more moderate role in world affairs and provides a credible alternative to a war-weary public—wide sectors of which have been seized by a mood of withdrawal from international politics. Although his Administration has not failed to prove its commitment to

European security in words or deeds, Europeans consider that this commitment would have the desired degree of long-term certainty only when it is not challenged domestically but is, instead, based on a dependable consensus. This consensus becomes all the more important if it should be decided to reduce the physical presence of the United States in Europe and reorganize certain aspects of the alliance.

The final assessment and restatement of any security commitment to Europe is, of course, an exclusively American matter, but discussions with Europeans, *e.g.,* within the proposed European-American Commission, would be desirable prior to decisions on this question. Any restatement of the American security commitment to Europe cannot be taken in isolation; it must depend not only on a common assessment of the security situation but also on possible future measures, particularly on the long-term contribution which Europe is willing to make. In view of the desirability of legislative action, participation by legislators in this consultative process would be desirable.

One possible form for the restatement of the security commitment between America and Europe would be a joint declaration by the participating governments, preferably on the occasion of the proposed summit meeting of heads of Atlantic governments. Such a declaration could be accompanied by appropriate declarations by the various legislatures, *e.g.,* in the United States by a "Sense of the Senate." Though declarations by the legislatures might differ from each other, each could relate to the basic issues covered in the governmental declaration.

A second possible approach would be to treat this declaration as a formal amendment to the NATO Treaty and to seek legislative action through the usual procedure of ratification.

Such a statement or amendment to the NATO Treaty should include a brief assessment of the common security situation prevailing after the 20-year period for which the original North Atlantic Treaty was concluded. Further developing the theme of the Harmel Report of 1968, the statement should outline the desirability of both security and détente and the prerequisites for each in both American and European policy. These prerequisites should include on the American side a mutual contribution to security, the nuclear guarantee, and a continued U.S. military presence in Western Europe. The statement could outline the common goals of policy on détente, arms control, and disarmament in Europe.

As with the NATO Treaty, the commitments undertaken in the common declaration should be valid for 15-20 years, and each side should agree to make important changes in its security policy only in coordination with its trans-Atlantic partners, or partner, once Europe can act as a single unit.

A European-American Financial Agreement

If Europeans conclude that their security will continue to depend on an American commitment to Europe and a physical military presence, they should make an effort to ease the financial burden of that commitment. Conversely, if the Americans conclude that the defense of Western Europe is in their national interest, they should likewise agree to bear a large part of the financial burden.

Americans who argue that the U.S. presence in Europe is a favor to Europeans who should consequently pay for it misread the realities of common security—in the same way as Europeans who argue that the cost of American troops in Europe is none of Europe's business, since it is incurred in pursuit of U.S. national interest. These kinds of arguments and continuous debate over sharing the financial burden have caused considerable strain in European-American relations and should be terminated by an agreement which settles such issues for a long time.

A relatively effective way of easing the financial problems of European-American security relations would be to carry out successful force reductions in East and West through MBFR. If one accepts the figure of $3 billion per year (operational, investment, and indirect costs), as the total cost of all U.S. forces stationed in Western Europe including the Mediterranean, a reduction of 40,000 troops in the first phase of MBFR as proposed above would amount to a saving for the United States of approximately $390 million annually. This calculation assumes that the units would be disbanded after their withdrawal.

Nor are the foreign exchange savings negligible. Unfortunately, it is difficult to give precise figures since expenditures vary according to the type of troops to be reduced and according to possible arrangements concerning reinforcement. (Should the materiel of the troops being reduced stay in Europe? At whose expense? Who pays for the transport capacity needed to assure reinforcement?) But if we take the 1971 foreign exchange costs for U.S. forces in Belgium, the Netherlands, and West Germany—amounting to $765 million ($1.24 billion minus $475 million of military purchases)—the proposed troop reduction would cut foreign exchange costs to approximately $350-400 million annually. These figures do not include the approximately $90 million which West Germany pays annually to the U.S. for troop facilities in the Federal Republic as a result of the 1971-73 U.S.-German Offset Agreement. Further savings would be made if in the second—but more difficult—phase of MBFR, a reduction of American troops or weapons can be negotiated.

Despite these potential benefits some difficult problems remain. Since the largest part of American troop expenditure in Europe is made in Germany, the United States has negotiated agreements with the German government whereby its foreign exchange expenditures have usually been offset about 80% by actions by the German government. In the beginning, this was done primarily by purchasing military equipment in the United States. Later, after the dollar weakened, it was achieved by German commitments not to change dollars into gold and to grant low-interest loans to the United States.

Both procedures have become increasingly difficult as Germany's needs for military equipment from the United States declined with the completion of rearmament and with growing pressure for standardization and production of arms within Europe. Moreover, the granting of loans to the United States by the German Central Bank postpones but does not solve the problem. As a result, in the 1971-73 Offset Agreement Germany agreed to pay $200 million to the United States to build and improve local facilities for U.S. troops.

In order to meet American criticisms of lagging European contributions, NATO also decided in December, 1970 to spend an additional $1 billion over five years on a European Defense Improvement Program for NATO infrastructure.

An attempt to reconcile American interests with European policies and financial capabilities in the light of the changing security situation could be made at two levels. At one, the financial implications of the U.S. security commitment to Europe must be seen in the context of the economic and monetary situation of the free world. Reform of the international monetary system and to a lesser extent of the international trade system must create preconditions for ending the chronic U.S. balance of payments deficit. If the non-Communist countries succeed in this, and Europe's contribution will be vital, part of the problem of easing the financial burden of American security policy in Europe will have been solved.

Europeans are divided on the question as to whether reform of the international economic system and American military involvement in Europe, should be connected. Some French argue that the United States may exploit the security issue in order to extract economic concessions from Europe, but other Europeans tend to accept a link between the two areas and see the need to help the American government find a solution acceptable to a highly sensitized American public, which overrates the economic burden of American military presence in Europe.

In any event, reform of the international economic system with its beneficial effects on the American balance of payments will not occur for some time. For this reason, intermediate measures should be considered.

At a second level, measures should be considered which could take effect very soon and be relatively permanent. Here we must distinguish between two things: First, an initial agreement on specific steps which Europe would take as long as the U.S. has a deficit balance of payments. This agreement could be framed as a semi-automatic obligation on Europe's part to help, through available monetary and other means, in solving what are, hopefully, only temporary difficulties.

A second agreement on the distribution of costs is more important, since possible troop reductions and savings can reduce the foreign exchange problem to more manageable proportions. Western Europe and America should together examine which expenditures in Europe can be taken over by Europeans as a group. If it is in the interest of all West Europeans to secure American involvement in Europe, then all should participate in such a scheme. Costs to be considered might include expenditures for the European infrastructure and could be financed, as well as administered, by an emerging West European defense establishment.

Measures aimed at a redistribution of costs would constitute an important step toward creation of a West European defense structure within the Alliance. The infrastructure such a group might take over includes, for example, supply and logistics, alert systems, radar installations, and billeting facilities for foreign troops. The last item is particularly important since a solution of this kind would transfer to a European pool the politically disadvantageous budgetary subsidy now paid by Germany for troop billeting. Financing this agreement, while multilateralizing a number of bilateral and NATO agreements, should not radically change the present distribution of costs.

The Creation of a West European Defense Structure

Strengthening a West European defense structure would be desirable for many reasons.[41] The time has come to create a stronger European identity within the Atlantic alliance and to make Europe's contribution not the sum of efforts by various states but a joint undertaking. Such a group would attempt to establish common positions whenever European interests are at stake or a European point of view is appropriate. It would work toward standardization and integration of arms production and establish a European command structure where feasible. The creation of such a group should facilitate and contribute to the emergence of a common European foreign policy.

Secondly, the establishment of a West European defense structure should help to maintain firm ties between the United States and Europe by reorganizing the relationship. It should supplant the old Atlantic Community, in which a powerful United States was associated with many smaller countries, with a partnership aimed at maintaining security and at creating the conditions required for peaceful change in Europe over the next decade.

Third, such a structure would help compensate for any military weakening of Western Europe as a result of troop reductions. It would also be the group to assume certain functions which the United States, in redefining her own role, might pass on to Western Europe.

Finally, such a structure would create better conditions for associating France more completely with the security efforts of Western Europe.

A West European defense structure could take the Euro-Group within NATO as a point of departure and develop it further. In a number of cases such measures might require agreements which, step by step, could give a more formal structure to the Group. The West European defense structure would be the appropriate forum for a

---

[41] The following proposals incorporate some suggestions made in Duchêne, "A New European Defense Community," op. cit.

number of activities connected with a European-American financial agreement, such as supply and logistics, communications, alert systems, and stationing of foreign troops. It could function as an equal partner with the United States and Canada and administer and finance such activities.

Although the West European defense group is not identical with an enlarged European Community which, already plagued with problems, should not be burdened with over-ambitious defense responsibilities, a pragmatic and gradually increasing association between the defense structure and European economic and political unification would be desirable. A first step in this direction could be made if the members of the group were to merge their permanent representations to the European Community and NATO.

After consolidation and development of arrangements with the United States and Canada, a West European defense structure might also be the appropriate, if not indispensable, mechanism for keeping any movement toward British-French cooperation in the nuclear field from having a decisive impact on Western Europe. Rather, it could induce further integration in this field. A number of technical, economic, and political reasons argue for cooperation between, and a merger of, these two deterrents. But the time is not yet ripe for this.[42] Cooperation or merger of the two forces, involving British transfer of nuclear know-how originating in the United States, would require American approval, and that approval is uncertain. Moreover, spokesmen for France, who have long stressed that the nuclear risk is indivisible and that a nation cannot delegate decisions on nuclear matters to others, argue that a merger of nuclear forces would require a degree of political unity far beyond what exists today.

---

[42] For a comprehensive analysis, see Ian Smart, "Future Conditional: The Prospect for Anglo-French Nuclear Cooperation," *Adelphi Papers*, No. 78 (London: The Institute for Strategic Studies, 1971).

Europe would be well-advised for many years to avoid the potentially divisive and controversial question of a common nuclear deterrent. But the time may come when a small but effective British-French deterrent would be useful, assuming a European role agreed on in the European Community and complementing the nuclear guarantee of the United States, which would support it. A West European defense structure could help prepare the ground for such a development and to prevent tension between Britain and France, on the one hand, and the rest of the European Community, particularly West Germany, on the other.

More than in the past there will be differences in perspectives and interests between the United States and Western Europe in the nuclear as well as the conventional field. This will be true, for example, in the field of arms control in Europe, such as MBFR. Nevertheless in view of European aspirations and the basic tenets of the Nixon Doctrine, Americans and Europeans should in the future regard a West European preoccupation with its own interests and positions as natural.

Progress toward European defense will depend primarily on the willingness of Europeans to coordinate and pool their resources and to give that coordination an increasingly political character as substance transcends technical matters. Secondly, as revealed by the unfortunate episode of the MLF in the 1960's, a unified European defense will require American backing as long as Europe's dependence on United States military support gives the American government leverage to impose its will on a European ally. (This remains true even though the long-term damage caused to European-American relations by such a course would be considerable, even more today than in the 1960's.)

It is imperative therefore that Americans and Europeans see the development of a separate European identity in defense matters against the background of common basic interests and make sure that its development does not lessen cooperation, particularly in the field of security.

A final word should be said about possible Soviet reaction. It will almost certainly not be positive. Since a development of this kind does not entail any overt provocation of the Soviet Union, her reaction may be relatively mild. Soviet interest in preventing sudden and potentially destabilizing changes in Europe was demonstrated earlier when Brezhnev's Tiflis speech favoring MBFR helped to defeat the Mansfield Amendment stipulating unilateral U.S. troop withdrawals. Creation of a West European defense structure can also be seen as an attempt to induce gradual change without upsetting fundamentally the existing East-West security structure. Since the establishment of a structure along the lines proposed could help to prevent the creation of a European nuclear force— the development feared most by the Soviet Union—she might well desist from opposing a Western European defense structure.

Of highest importance is the general context of détente within which such a group is formed. If its development accompanies troop reductions in Europe, negotiations about further arms control and various ventures in East-West cooperation, its political explosiveness will largely be defused. Much depends on Western willingness genuinely to cooperate in measures of arms control in Europe. If this cooperation is demonstrated, the Soviet Union might not strongly oppose creation of what the West European defense structure really should be, namely, "a minimum insurance against a breakdown of détente." [43]

SALT II AND MBFR II

There is no doubt that the United States and Europe have a common interest in curbing the arms race and lowering the risk of war and the cost of arms. While East-West agreements of the last 10 years, including the Test Ban

---

[43] Duchêne, "A New European Defense Community," op. cit., p. 81.

Treaty, the Non-Proliferation Treaty, the Seabeds Treaty, and the SALT Agreement, do not yet add up to the kind of qualitative change that mankind needs in the arms race, each of these agreements represents progress.

Especially the SALT Agreement between the Soviet Union and the United States represents a step forward, and has been acclaimed by all of America's allies in Europe. This agreement to limit anti-ballistic and offensive missiles is the first instance in which two great opposing powers have accepted a restriction of their strategic weapons. The enhancement of military security for both also represents a gain for Europe since it serves to reduce the risk of war. But the real importance of the agreement lies in the fact that it was "part of a larger decision to place relations on a new foundation of restraint, cooperation, and steadily evolving confidence," [44] hence, in its positive impact on political relations between the two super-powers.[45]

Europeans who overlook the security gains of the agreement interpret it as a step toward superpower collusion in dividing the world between themselves. This view neglects two important facts. Despite efforts at restraint and cooperation, both powers will remain ideological adversaries for a long time. They will compete politically and militarily and try to oppose significant advances by the other over their respective allies or vital areas. Secondly, any measure of improvement in political relations and cooperation between the two superpowers helps

---

[44] Henry A. Kissinger, in a Congressional Briefing on the SALT Agreement, June 15, 1972, *White House Press Release,* mimeographed.

[45] The critics of the first SALT Agreements usually underrate this political dimension in U.S.-Soviet relations when they make the point that the agreements do not curb the qualitative arms race but may even accelerate it (for that very reason the second round of SALT will deal with qualitative questions) and that the action-reaction analysis of armament and arms control such as SALT underestimates the domestic autonomy of armament. See: Dieter Senghaas, *Aufrüstung durch Rüstungskontrolle. Über den symbolischen Gebrauch von Politik* (Stuttgart: Kohlhammer, 1972).

Europe since it may reduce competition in Europe and enhance the possibility of cooperative links between East and West.

The second phase of SALT, which began in October 1972, may be of even greater importance to the West Europeans since it could directly affect their own interests as well as relations with the United States. If SALT II confines itself to examining the highly complex questions of technological change, quality and means of verification of offensive missiles—repetition of the bilateral American-Soviet negotiations, accompanied by a constant flow of information to the West European Allies on all developments, as practiced in SALT I, would be satisfactory to the West Europeans.

But should the Soviet Union want to discuss other weapons systems such as bombers, tactical nuclear weapons, MBRMs, and general naval forces, West Europeans would be anxious to participate in the negotiations. Measures undertaken in these areas are likely to affect the arms situation in Europe, the nature of America's security guarantee, the validity of current European strategy, and the internal structure of the alliance.

Since joint security requires joint arms control, negotiations on these issues should be multilateral. Moreover, except for issues which remain a bilateral American-Soviet matter, an enlarged SALT II should be linked with MBFR since both obviously concern a number of overlapping subjects.

Such a linkage of SALT II and MBFR II would, of course, raise the problem of an appropriate negotiating procedure. one that will remain effective despite the large number of participants involved in discussion of the multilateral issues. Perhaps the task can be facilitated by trying to develop mechanisms among the Europeans and between the Americans and Europeans for establishing common negotiating positions, even though this procedure would take more time. Such an approach would meet the growing desire to establish collective European positions on some issues. It should be obvious at the very least that Europe and America need to coordinate positions before and during the negotiations.

In MBFR II, all the subjects mentioned above in the section on the first phase should be put on the negotiating table. Because immensely complex issues must be settled in package deals in order to achieve balanced results, MBFR II is likely to become a continuing process. Each step can do little more than reflect in arms control terms the respective stage of political evolution between East and West. For this reason, arms control measures will largely depend on the success of concrete cooperative ventures between East and West.

4. The United States and the European Community

American attitudes toward the emerging European Community have changed considerably in recent years. Our earlier analysis of various issues in the fields of economics and security traced this change from unconditional support in the early post-war period, to a mixture of qualified support at the official level, and indifference, misgivings, and opposition at the unofficial level. Moreover, the nature of the issues dividing the United States and Europe and the dynamics of the forces in play suggest that this U.S.-European alienation may become worse unless both sides make energetic efforts to reorganize their relationship.

Such reorganization should aim at restructuring relations along the lines of a bilateral partnership, with special machinery for consultation and policy coordination.

The Necessity for European Unity

The present inability of the European Community to overcome its national divisions and to move toward genuine economic and political union is one of the major reasons for rising American reservations about the European

Community. The revival of genuine effort toward unification will make an important difference to both the United States and others in evaluating the Community's economic impact on themselves.

Greater unity is necessary also for greater effectiveness in solving common problems. As indicated above, the United States and Europe must undertake thorough reform in many fields. The chances of success will be infinitely greater if instead of the frustrations of dealing with nine different nations the United States can deal with one single partner—a Europe which can express itself with one voice, regardless of whether it is the Commission of the Community or a particular member of the Community speaking for the whole.

If the European Community fails to make substantial progress toward unification within the near future, American resistance to certain economic measures adopted by the Community is likely to grow, along with American disillusionment with a movement which they had supported for many years with great hope. A tougher American policy in its dealings with nine divided countries could, of course, aggravate Europeans' resentment over their inferior situation and make them turn against the United States, leaving American policy torn between the choice of withdrawal and continuing involvement to protect its own interests.

The Difficult Path Toward Partnership

The degree of mutual misunderstanding, lack of information, and ignorance of the fundamental problems at stake has reached a dangerous level in European-American relations. As a European observer put it, "American opinion tends to perceive simultaneously the spectacular 'reconciliation' with China, the partial arrangements with the Soviet Union, and the monetary commercial quarrels with the Europeans; it appears as if the United States had as adversaries, if not as enemies, allies only." [46]

A rational debate is needed on the issues at stake in which problems are examined, illusions and prejudices exposed, and alternatives presented. Unless, for example, the informed American public can be convinced through a rational presentation of the facts that U.S. isolationism and protectionism are basically not in America's interest, any attempt to reform trade or monetary policy, let alone security policy, will be difficult if not futile. Therefore, a public discussion to accompany measures at the diplomatic level between America and Europe is urgently necessary.

We have already outlined in some detail the policy measures needed in various fields. In the field of security we need a reassessment and restatement of the mutual commitment, combined with efforts to maintain a reduced American presence in Europe and reorganization of the trans-Atlantic security relationship through creation of a West European defense structure.

In economics, we suggested various areas where both sides have a common stake in reform and in establishing an effective new system for managing the interdependent international economy. Though most of these steps will require coordination with Japan, as well as the establishment of institutions in a larger framework consisting of the major industrialized countries of the West, there can be no reform without contributions by the United States and Europe. Their leadership will be decisive in approaching the multitude of problems to be solved in the coming years.

In the political field, the success of new rounds of negotiations with the Socialist states on arms control and cooperation in Europe will depend to a large extent on the ability of the West, with the United States and the Euro-

[46] Raymond Aron, *Vingt-cinq ans après le Plan Marshall,* paper given at an American-European Conference at Royaumont, May 4-7, 1972, mimeographed, p. 27.

pean Community at its center, to develop and implement a coordinated strategy.

The tasks ahead are huge and the stakes enormous. What significantly distinguishes America's relations with Europe (as well as American-Japanese relations) from her relations with the Soviet Union and China—although these are sometimes mentioned in ways which suggest that they are similar—is an underlying identity of interest in all major political and economic areas as well as a traditional predisposition toward cooperation.

To mobilize this tradition of cooperation and activate a common interest in approaching future problems will be the task of statesmen in America and Europe. Each side will depend on the other for effective policies in a variety of fields. And each will face the difficult task of safeguarding its own identity within an interdependent relationship.

President Nixon's "State of the Nation" Message of 1972 remarked on this problem: "This change means the end of American tutelage and the end of the era of automatic unity. But discord is not inevitable either. The challenge to our maturity and political skill is to establish a new practice in Atlantic unity—finding common ground in a consensus of independent policies instead of in deference to American prescriptions." [47]

In dealing with nine European countries which are engaged in the difficult process of integration, the United States will inevitably make certain decisions which will affect the process of unification. If America does not wish to repeat the stand taken by the Kennedy Administration, which made acceptance of Europe as a partner dependent upon completion of unity, and thereby postponed the partnership, the U.S. government should treat the emerging Community as one unit in its day-to-day dealings, even if unity is only partial and still in the process of attainment.

---

[47] *U.S. Foreign Policy for the 1970's, op. cit.,* p. 40.

Towards Coordinated Regional Policies?

The European Community and the United States are both becoming aware of the fundamental changes occurring in world politics. Separately, they are beginning to argue about and conceptualize the future structure of international politics. But there has not been so far any attempt at a common review of the future they will share under growing conditions of interdependence.

There is a striking absence of consultation or integrated views on various regional problems in world politics of vital importance to the European Community, Japan, and the United States. Only partial aspects of some regional problems, such as military dimensions or a specific problem arising from some country's trade policy, become the subject of consultation. An attempt must be made to review the problems of a region multilaterally, in a comprehensive way, and to discuss possible approaches that may be made in common. Three regions are pertinent.

A Mediterranean Policy

The most striking example of a neglected area vital to Europe which has been a possible subject for comprehensive review and consultation among Europeans and between Americans and Europeans is obviously the Mediterranean. This region is growing in importance to both the United States and the European Community for two basic reasons.

First, it is fraught with present and potential conflicts. The Arab-Israeli conflict will probably remain the dominant tension in the region. Contrary to the relatively stable situation in Central and Northern Europe, wars have broken out here and may break out again. Conflicts may be found throughout the Mediterranean Basin, including the continuing tension between Turkey and Greece over Cyprus; potential domestic instability in Greece, Spain, and Turkey; the uncertain future of some Arab states, such as Morocco and Saudi Arabia; internal Arab disputes and tensions, such as those between Algeria and Morocco and between Jordan and her neighbors; and, finally, the uncertain future of multi-ethnic Yugoslavia, delicately poised between East and West in an area traditionally ridden with ethnic tensions and instability.

Secondly, the growing energy demands of Western Europe, the United States, and Japan will make these areas increasingly dependent on oil imports from the Middle East. In no other way will their complex industrial societies be so economically vulnerable. This was brought home to Europe during the Suez Crisis but the consequences of a cut-off from Near East oil today or in the future would be infinitely more serious. The United States would suffer equally, although U.S. public awareness of America's growing dependence on oil imports still lags behind the facts. It is a hard fact that the functioning of the Western industrialized societies has become dependent on imports from one of the world's most unstable areas.

Current failure to review these problems comprehensively, to seek common policies or to undertake contingency planning is a major example of short-sightedness on the part of Western countries. It amounts to a brinkmanship which we can no longer afford.

Of course there have been some attempts at common review and consultation. The attempt by the European Community to arrive at a common position on the Arab-Israeli conflict, and NATO's contingency planning for this area (lacking, however, French participation, which would be vital in any crisis) are examples. But a comprehensive review of the problems of this area is urgently required. It must take place at a high level, with competent expert advice which integrates the various relevant issues, ranging from the strategic importance of trade agreements with Mediterranean countries to a policy on the Arab-Israeli conflict, contingency planning for specific crises arising from upheavals in different parts of the Mediterranean, and emergency plans in the event of a rupture in oil supplies.

This comprehensive review should be undertaken on a pragmatic basis which does not pose problems of participation by any vital state, *e.g.,* France in the European context, and Canada and Japan in a wider context. Obviously, Japan and Canada would be indispensable partners in the review of the oil problem.

An Understanding on Africa

In earlier discussion of preferential agreements, it was concluded that the United States and the European Community should not allow the Community's preferential arrangements with Africa to remain a constant source of friction.

The European Community, Japan, and the United States should undertake a comprehensive review of preferential agreements within the context of a general policy on problems of development and world order. Of course, if the proposal for complete removal of all tariffs within 10 years is realized, the problem of preferential treatments would lose much of its relevance, though the question of quantitative restrictions will be posed all the more sharply.

Assuming that a removal of tariffs will eliminate the basic threat of preferential agreements to the Most Favored Nation treatment as a basis for international trade, the European Community has no reason to be defensive about its association agreements with African states. Their main purpose is to help these states in their efforts at development. The Yaounde Convention constitutes Europe's own little Marshall Plan for Africa.

When Britain joined the Community, it became official policy to offer association agreements to virtually all the states of Africa. The East African states have already taken up this offer and have concluded an association agreement. An extension of the association to African states generally solves some problems and raises new ones. It could help to overcome the age-old division of Africa into English-speaking and French-speaking countries. At the same time it may enhance the inequality of treatment among underdeveloped nations.

The European Community, Japan, and the United States should have a frank exchange of views on this problem. Should it become their long-term policy to eliminate their special spheres of influence in the underdeveloped world? Is the United States willing to abandon the idea that Latin America represents her special area of responsibility and cooperation as expresed *inter alia* by such arrangements as the Alliance for Progress and the OAS? Should the European Community, Japan, and the United States agree on a policy, attenuating over a period of years, of discriminatory treatment of developing countries according to regions while simultaneously accepting the notion that each of them has regional development responsibilities which will complement aid actions by multilateral institutions and other countries?

Consultations on Asia

Asia, today undergoing far-reaching change, should be a third area for consultation. Besides discussing the long-term strategic implications of changing Asiatic power relationships, consultation should cover American, European, and Japanese trade and economic relations with China and the possibilities of joint cooperative ventures with the Soviet Union for the development of Siberia.

Unfortunately there is no forum for discussion of such long-term questions of political strategy. While some of these questions could be taken up in connection with international economic reform, others should be discussed at the political level.

The time has come for the European Community, Japan, and the United States to review possible strategies for the future at a high political level, thus complementing their common attempts to reform the international economic system. Such a common assessment of the present situation and of policies for the future should cover all basic elements pertaining to international stability as well as the changing structure of the international system.

Preconditions and Machinery for Communication and Coordination

Despite increasing interaction in many fields between Europe and North America, on each side there is considerable lack of knowledge about the other, the facts of its existence, its perceptions, and priorities. In view of the urgency and complexity of the problems which lie ahead, the United States and Europe need more effective communication and policy coordination as they enter a new phase in restructuring international politics. The preconditions and the machinery that are needed are either absent or insufficient in four areas.

First, inter-governmental communication does not function well enough in the area of policy-making. In America the divergency between policies of different departments poses some problems, but the major problem arises from the absence of a clear partner to communicate within Europe. Consultations between the United States and the Commission of the European Community, as they take place today on a regular basis, are useful but insufficient. Intensive and regular communication is absolutely essential to keep each other informed and to eliminate minor causes of friction and misunderstanding.

There is urgent need, therefore, to establish some kind of machinery for continuous communication between the United States Government and the European Community. This task could be assigned either to the Commission, which should possess a sufficiently broad mandate to be able to carry it out, or to a representative of the Council of Ministers, or both. Such machinery must be accompanied by a commitment from both sides to consult and inform the other about specific problems as a means of avoiding unilateral surprise decisions which affect the interests of the other side.[48] Such machinery would complement the existing channels for bilateral and multilateral communication with OECD or NATO.

Second, effective trans-Atlantic communication between the élites relevant for foreign policy is declining. Both in Europe and America many of the élites, who maintained effective communication in the past, are gradually being eliminated from the foreign policy-making as a result of age and a restructuring of the foreign policy mechanism. Trans-Atlantic communication among legislators, never very intensive in the post-war period, has declined even further.

Moreover, the European Community does not sufficiently explain itself to the Americans. Except for a small number, the American élite—to say nothing of the general public—know almost nothing about what goes on in the Community.

As America and Europe enter a phase of restructuring their mutual relations and their role in the world, it is absolutely crucial that a minimum of communication be revived among legislators and other members of the political élite who will influence this process. This is all the more needed since the reform measures to be negotiated and implemented in coming years cannot remain the prerogative of executive branches in Europe and America; a consensus of legislatures and the public will be required in support of the new policies. The time has come therefore for legislators and private groups on both sides of the Atlantic to make a deliberate effort to increase communication and discussion among themselves.

This leads us to a third subject: Public awareness of and involvement in the process of reform. Public debate on both sides of the Atlantic, involving a rational assessment of the situation, the presentation of factual information, and a statement of available alternatives must be

---

[48] See in this connection the proposals made by Robert Schaetzel, *op. cit.*

promoted to create a democratic consensus behind any reform measures. Ignorance or misconceptions cloud many of the relevant issues. In the United States, where the building of domestic consensus behind a restructured foreign policy is particularly urgent, television, radio, and most newspapers fail to provide adequate information about the rest of the world, let alone qualified analyses or examinations of possible foreign policy alternatives.

For these reasons, private groups and foundations on both sides of the Atlantic should make a major effort to provide at least minimal information about the other side and to encourage discussion and the presentation of rational alternatives on policy issues. They have an opportunity to help build domestic consensus behind needed new measures in relations between the United States and Europe as well as behind common contributions to reform in international politics.

The fourth and final subject is, in essence, a special manifestation of the third—attitudes among the young. European and American governments and foreign policy élites must make a more deliberate effort to confront the young with foreign policy problems and alternatives. At the moment every analysis made of youth in America and Europe today points to the same conclusions.

The more educated members of the younger generation tend either to withdraw entirely from any interest in foreign policy or to oppose it, on the grounds that foreign policy stabilizes domestic arrangements they would like to change. Alternatively, foreign policy is seen entirely in moralistic terms, with attention focused exclusively on the Third World's liberation movements or development. The concerns of policy-makers on both sides of the Atlantic are regarded simply as irrelevant. Another less educated, less vocal, and less involved segment of the younger generation may share some of the concerns of foreign policy-makers, but usually conceives international politics in a crude, conservative fashion as a struggle in which the strongest survive.

It is not satisfactory to reply that the younger generation is not specially relevant to foreign policy-making or that the socialization process of élite recruitment will assure continuity. A continuation of the present rift between the educated, vocal younger generation and the foreign policy élite not only generates continuous tension in domestic politics in some countries but is likely to affect foreign policy as a result of the growing impact of this younger group on public opinion generally.

A conscious effort is needed by governments and foreign policy élites on both sides of the Atlantic to engage in a rational dialogue with the younger generation on foreign policy issues, however painful and difficult this may be. The most important factor in creating interest in, and consensus behind, foreign policy is, of course, the policy itself—its persuasiveness and credibility, its concern for developing countries, and its ability to create better conditions for peace.

5. The Development Problem

For the European Community, Japan and the United States, particularly prosperous countries and major aid donors, the problem of development has been a major concern. They will be forced to give even greater attention to this problem in future years. First, the problem of underdevelopment and relations with underdeveloped countries are linked to various issues which must be discussed in connection with reform of the international economic system. Second, a number of trends discussed below suggest that the development problem is likely to become more urgent within the next few years, impelling the advanced nations to become more active in this field.

Aggravating Trends in the Development Problem

The gap between the rich and the poor countries has widened despite substantial aid by the industrialized countries and the remarkable growth in the underdeveloped countries during the Development Decade that ended in 1970. Although the target growth of 5% of the GNP was exceeded, a large part of this gain was neutralized by the unprecedented rate of population growth in most developing countries in the 1960's, averaging almost 2.5% per year. The gap between rich and poor countries has widened both relatively and absolutely. While income in the developing states rose about $10 per head during the decade, it rose by about $300 in the industrial countries.

Moreover, the developing countries went ever deeper into debt—about $50 billion, of which half must be repaid by 1975. The private and public debts of developing countries have reached such proportions that debt service now amounts to between 50% and 85% of new loan dispersements in many cases. In most developing countries, the debt problem has assumed genuine crisis proportions.

Modest progress is over-shadowed by the deepening of inequalities among social groups inside developing countries.

Despite many hopeful signs, the pace of progress in these countries is so frustratingly slow and the perception of the widening gap so intense that instability and militancy are very likely to increase in the years ahead.

The environmental problem almost certainly adds further strains to relations between developed and underdeveloped countries. The additional cost of pollution-free industrial equipment, which industrialized nations will increasingly insist on, is likely to exceed the probable small increase in development aid and, as a result, will, de facto, decrease its productive impact. Pollution and health standards, which will become much more stringent in the industrialized countries, will also affect some exports from developing countries. It is by no means certain that they will be completely compensated for resulting losses. Developing countries understandably object to being deprived of industrialization, having not yet reaped either its rewards or its penalties, simply because northern countries, already rich, no longer want to live with its ill effects.

The growing strains between developed and developing countries, clearly apparent, for example, at the 1972 U.N. Conference on Trade and Development in Santiago, will not make it easier to formulate a rational development policy. But the European Community, the United States, and Japan have a considerable stake and responsibility in taking into account the interests of the developing world when they set out to reorganize their own relations.

Reform of the International Economy and Development

Most of the issues involved in reform of the international economic system have a development aspect. Since no ready-made answers are available about how the interests of the developing countries can best be served, it is essential that the European Community and the United States make an effort to include them in a common review of possible solutions.

Thus, any joint review of possible monetary reform should both give developing countries a full voice in the discussions and examine how a new system might better assist them. This particularly applies to credit facilities in connection with SDR's.

The Community, Japan, and the United States should also examine the desirability for all concerned of continuing the present system of preferential agreements with African and Mediterranean countries—a system which could ultimately result in three regional spheres of influence involving Europe, the United States, and Japan. In any event, a complete removal of tariffs, combined with the lifting of quotas for goods from developing countries, would offer the kind of trading opportunities which developing countries need. In discussions of possible adjustment procedures, one would have to consider what special allowances might be made for developing countries.

Developing countries would also be especially interested in a possible agreement on rules regarding multinational corporations since these are seen as having powerful political and economic implications and, in some cases, as being threats to their independence. But the interests of the advanced and developing worlds differ so greatly on this subject that a case could be made for working out an agreement on multinational corporations within the industrialized world first, and dealing with the problem in developing countries separately, in a second round of negotiations.

Environment and Development

The finiteness of our world and its resources necessitates far-reaching adaptations in our economic and social policies in order to deal effectively with the environment. If we examine the consequences of the environmental problem for developing countries, the possible implications are no less intriguing than for industrialized nations. If environment is considered in a worldwide context, the reasons for modifying policies in industrialized nations become even more compelling.

Our past concept of development has been one in which the industrialized world continues to grow and become richer while the underdeveloped world, through a massive transfer of aid and the application of technology, grows even faster so that the gap between rich and poor constantly becomes narrower. But if we actually succeed in raising the living standard of the five billion people who will live in the underdeveloped world in the Year 2000 to, approximately, the level of Japan, a drastic depletion of the world's resources, catastrophic forms of pollution (especially in connection with agricultural technology), and major disruptions would result.

At the same time it is inhuman to deny economic growth to the underdeveloped countries. Many ardent advocates of zero growth have not faced up to the moral implications of their view insofar as the Third World is concerned. For economic advancement is essential in solving the problem of underdevelopment.

Is there no possible course between two unacceptable extremes: Denial of development or the prospect of possible environmental catastrophes? "We are left with the absolute necessity of a third course: The purposive development in the Third World of sustainable standards of nutrition, schooling, widely shared incomes, and, above all, labor—absorbing agriculture and industry on the one hand and, on the other, the equally purposive development in the rich countries of standards which are more intellectually, artistically, and spiritually rich and less consumptive in materials and energy." [49] Such a course requires fundamental re-thinking of existing development models which, in most cases, merely repeat the wasteful patterns of the industrialized North. This course is likely to meet with strong resistance in the developing countries. Such a shift, which most of these countries see as a sacrifice, would be acceptable to them only if the industrialized countries contributed in turn to a more rational use of existing resources—and that is an immensely difficult task.

It is difficult to assess the immediate implications of the environmental problem for the development policy of the European Community, Japan, and the United States. We have just begun to think about these problems. Diplomats and politicians at the recent U.N. Conference on the Environment in Stockholm were mainly concerned, for example, with the "traditional" questions of transfer of resources, payment for additional costs of anti-pollution devices, compensation for possible export losses as a result of new standards, etc.

Much could be said for another "Pearson Commission" which would thoroughly examine possible implications

---

[49] Lady Jackson (Barbara Ward) in a letter of March 3, 1972, to the author.

of the environmental problem for the development policies of both industrial and developing nations.

The End of Aid Increase?

Although the environmental problem casts a shadow of uncertainty on the future direction of development policy, the massive and increasing transfer of resources to the developing world continues to remain an utmost necessity. However, the record of aid to developing countries is not encouraging. In 1970, of the total increase of about 7%, half resulted from price inflation, and most of the increase was due to private export credits and investments. The really crucial aid, official development assistance, rose only 3%—just enough to keep up with price increases. Although official development assistance rose in absolute terms, from $4.6 to $6.8 billion, between 1960 and 1970, it decreased in relative terms, from 0.52% of GNP to 0.34%. In the same time span, the GNP of the OECD members doubled and governments increased their general expenditures from $156 billion in 1961 to $292 billion in 1970.

The governments of the industrialized countries of the West had previously agreed that development aid should not only grow in proportion to their own increase in wealth but faster, until a new flow of resources to developing countries, amounting to 1% of GNP, was attained. One can cite many reasons why aid expenditures, which had reached a figure of 0.95% in 1961, fell to 0.74% by 1970. Each of the donor governments must undertake costly domestic reforms in many areas.

But the fatalism with which Western policy-makers accept this downward trend in aid is profoundly disturbing. No doubt, given the public mood at present, one cannot gain votes in elections on the issue of development aid. But the public mood can be changed if political leaders choose to take a strong public stand on these important issues. Self-interest in a stable world and, above all, humanity demand a change of our policies.

6. The Future of European-American Relations

Most Europeans see the reelection of President Nixon as the electorate's mandate for prudent internationalism and gradualism in reassessing America's international role.

But if doubts remain among a minority of Europeans concerning the long-term prospects for the European-American security relationship, these stem from the realization that the burning nature of America's domestic problems, the probability of continued détente and the attitudes of many Americans, particularly youth, may make an American withdrawal from Europe inevitable. Some would even argue that it is "unhistorical" to assume that an American involvement in Europe could go on indefinitely.

Among the Europeans who believe that American disengagement is inevitable are a few who see a radical approach as the only hope. In their view (partly supported by American advocates of neo-isolationism [50]) the shock of sudden U.S. withdrawal would force the Europeans to unite and take their security into their own hands. But the overwhelming majority of thoughtful Europeans, while convinced that European unification is inevitable and necessary for a redistribution of security burdens, regard such a course as reckless. The cure might kill the patient, and Europe might be condemned to instability.

Another group of Europeans, undoubtedly the majority, does not share the fatalism of those who regard a lasting security relationship between the United States and Europe as "unhistorical." Surely, the present period sets new standards of history, and it would be short-sighted to restrict today's behavior to yesterday's rules. Only in a lost world of self-contained nations could America retire into its shell. But in today's world of nuclear weapons, when the cost of a break-down of security is so high as

---

[50] For example: Robert W. Tucker, *A New Isolationism: Threat or Promise?* (New York: Universe Books, 1972).

to be unacceptable, withdrawal is not a real option. Moreover, the multinational links of interdependence which intricately connect modern Western states and their economic and social welfare, do not allow a retreat into economic autarchy and isolation. Any such retreat from the realities of today would wreck the unprecedented post-war achievements of world prosperity and freedom of movement.

Measured by the new rules for maintaining peace in a nuclear world and managing interdependent relationships, why should it not be considered normal for the United States to be permanently involved in an international structure that preserves peace for Europe and herself?

It is high time that Americans and Europeans examine together long-term solutions for the problems plaguing their relationship. First priority must be given to prompt actions which will eliminate erosive tensions in the economic field. No long-term reform in the economic, political, and security fields will be possible if present economic tensions continue to undermine the cooperative basis of Western relations.

This analysis has tried to show in some detail the common problems faced by the United States and Western Europe. None of these problems is easy to solve, since they are either the outcome of incisive transformations or must be approached within the context of these transformations.

Just when interdependence is growing, Western societies, especially the United States, are turning inward to face their domestic problems. Therefore, a way must be found to make people perceive the exigencies of interdependence and seek rational solutions—despite the extraordinary range of built-in obstacles, narrow-minded lobbyists, and a disinterested public which prefers not to be bothered with difficult matters. The critical conditions in European-American relations are real, and we must make people face this crisis before it comes about.

The United States and Europe have always been able to coexist with conflict since differences in perspectives and interests are natural. Our problem now is to prevent existing conflicts from escalating into a permanent state of tension that could seriously undermine the cooperative nature of the Atlantic relationship.

Since the problems are fundamental, they cannot be settled by a technical approach but require a thorough assessment and policies that look beyond the immediate future. Neither the United States nor the European Community, given the many ways in which their fates are interwoven, can undertake such an effort alone (although there are some additional problems, resulting from the world role of the United States, in which Europe's contribution can at best be marginal). The United States and Europe should ask themselves how they can help each other to face the issues at stake. Both must make an effort to overcome present ignorance about the perceptions and priorities of the other. Both must lock themselves into long-term programs and policies that protect each against the parochial interests of the other.

This task deserves attention at the highest political level in Europe and the United States. Moreover, on many of these issues, notably international economic reform, the contribution of other Western states, particularly Japan, is vital. The United States and the European Community should consider how courageous political leadership can give momentum and guidance to this process.

The United States and Europe have no time to lose.

APPENDIX

Participants of Meetings in Europe and Columbia, Maryland, 1972

Albonetti, Achille, National Committee for Nuclear Energy, Rome

Aliboni, Roberto, Institute for International Affairs, Rome

Allison, Graham, Professor of Government, Harvard University, Cambridge

Anderson, Robert O., Chairman, Aspen Institute for Humanistic Studies, New York and Aspen, Colorado

Appell, Paul, President, Geigy-Ciba, Paris

Arena, Romolo, Department of International Relations, IRI, Rome

Arndt, Klaus-Dieter, former Under Secretary of Economic Affairs, Member of Parliament (SPD), Director, German Institute for Economic Research, Berlin

Aron, Raymond, Professor, College de France, Paris

Ball, George, former Under Secretary of State, New York

Barker, Paul, Editor, *New Society,* London

Berger, Marilyn, Diplomatic Correspondent, *The Washington Post,* Washington

Berlin, Sir Isaiah, Scholar and Head of Wolfson College, Oxford

Birrenbach, Kurt, Member of Parliament (CDU), and Chairman of the Board of the Thyssen Corporation and of the Thyssen Foundation, Düsseldorf

Bourlanges, Jean-Louis, Professor of Political Science, former secretary-general of a UDR group of parliamentarians, Paris

Brzezinski, Zbigniew, Herbert Lehman Professor of Government, and Director of the Research Institute on Communist Affairs, Columbia University, New York

Bullock, Sir Alan, Vice Chancellor, Oxford University, and Chairman, International Association for Cultural Freedom, London

Casadio, Gian Paolo, University of Bologna, Bologna

Cavazza, Fabio Luca, Editor, *Il Sole 24 Ore,* Milan

Cellitto, Franco, Institute for International Affairs, Rome

Cittadini-Cesi, Giangaspare, former Italian diplomat; President, Association pour l'Etude des Problèmes de l'Europe, Paris

Clément, Alain, former Washington correspondent of *Le Monde* and now roving correspondent and editorial writer, Paris

Conine, Ernest, Senior Editorial Writer, *The Los Angeles Times,* Los Angeles

Corterier, Peter, Member of Parliament (SPD), Bonn

de Jouvenel, Bertrand, Professor, economist, and planner, Paris

Dido, Mario, General Confederation of Labour of Italy, Rome

Dingels, Hans-Eberhard, Head of International Relations Section, Executive Committee, SPD, Bonn

Doenhoff, Marion, Countess, Publisher, *Die Zeit,* Hamburg

Doty, Paul, Professor, Harvard University

Duchêne, François, Director, International Institute for Strategic Studies, London

Düren, Albrecht, former Secretary General, German Chamber of Commerce, Bad Honnef

Emmanuel, Pierre, Président du Conseil du Developpement Culturel; Director of IACF, Paris

Ferraris, Luigi Vittorio, Ministry of Foreign Affairs, Rome

Flitner, Hugbert, Director, Fritz Thyssen Foundation, Cologne

Foulkes, Nigel, industrialist; Chairman, British Airports Authority, London

Franklin, George, Secretary Pro Tem, Trilateral Commission, New York

Galli, Giorgio, Giovanni Agnelli Foundation, Torino

Gardner, Richard N., Professor of Law, Columbia University, New York

Goldman, Guido, Acting President, The German Marshall Fund of the United States, Washington

Granelli, Luigi, Member of Parliament (DC), Rome

Hartley, Anthony, writer; Executive Director, Committee of Nine, North Atlantic Assembly, London

Hassner, Pierre, Professor of Political Science, Fondation Nationale des Sciences Politiques, Paris

Hatzfeldt, Hermann, economist, Schloss Crottorf Wissen-Sieg, Germany

Hoffmann, Stanley, Professor of Government, Harvard University

Holbrooke, Richard, Managing Editor, *Foreign Policy,* New York

Javits, Jacob K., United States Senator from New York (R), Washington

Jelenski, Constantin, Director of Seminars, IACF, Paris

Jenkins, Roy, Member of Parliament (L), London

Jordan, Amos A., Director, Aspen Institute for Humanistic Studies, New York and Aspen, Colorado

Kaiser, Karl, Professor of Political Science, University of the Saarland, Saarbruecken

Kirk, Peter, Member of Parliament (C), London

Kloten, Norbert, Professor of Economics, Chairman of German Council of Economic Advisors

Laqueur, Walter, Professor, Director, Institute of Contemporary History and Wiener Library, London

Lawson, Nigel, writer and columnist, *London Times,* London

Lemerle, Paul, Ministry of Foreign Affairs, Paris

Leuprecht, Peter, Head of Division, Office of the Clerk of the Assembly, Council of Europe, Strasbourg

Levi, Arrigo, Editor, *La Stampa,* Rome

Löwenthal, Richard, Professor of Political Science, Free University of Berlin, Berlin

Malfatti, Franco Maria, Member of Parliament (DC), Rome

Mander, John, author and contributor to *Encounter,* London

Martinet, Gilles, writer and a publisher of the *Nouvel Observateur,* Paris

Mathias, Charles McC., Jr., United States Senator from Maryland (R), Washington